OUTINGS IN

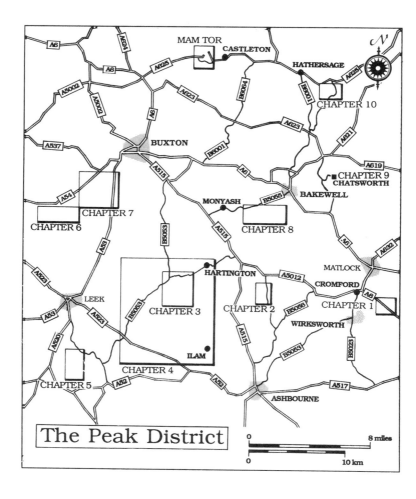

The Peak District

Outings

in the

Peak District

Graham Knight & Lindsey Porter

MPC

Published by:
Moorland Publishing Co Ltd,
Moor Farm Road,
Airfield Estate,
Ashbourne,
Derbyshire DE6 1HD
England

British Library Cataloguing in
Publication Data
Knight, Graham
    Outings in the Peak District.
    I. Title
    914.2504

    ISBN 0 86190 407 9

Black & White origination by:
Monochrome Scanning Ltd

Printed in the UK by:
Billings & Son Ltd, Worcester

Cover picture: The view from
Mam Tor towards Lose Hill,
with Stella Porter in the
foreground.

Illustration of Ilam Hall taken
from the book *Mrs Delany: Her
Life and Her Flowers* by Ruth
Hayden (British Museum
Publications).
All other illustrations are from
the MPC Picture Collection.

MPC Production Team:
Editor: Tonya Monk
Designer: Jonathan Moss
Cartographer: Alastair
Morrison

Contents

Key to Symbols
used in text and on maps

P	Car Park	*i*	Tourist Information
	Picnic Sites		Cycle Hire
	Toilets		Craft Shop
	Accommodation		Sports Facilities
	Places to Eat		Facilities for the Disabled

Note on the Maps
The maps drawn for each chapter while comprehensive, are not designed to be used as route maps but rather to locate main towns, villages and places of interest.

Introduction

T he Peak District National Park, established in 1951, receives some 22 million visitors per annum, making it the most visited national park in Europe. It is a truly remarkable number of people. Over 4 million people come to walk more than 2 miles while a similar number simply drive around.

Many of those walking in excess of 2 miles may be assumed to have a good knowledge of the area, or at least how to read a map. Clearly there are many other people whose knowledge is not so great. This book is for them! However, it is hoped that other lovers of the Peak will find it of value. *Outings in the Peak District* is more than just a walking book. Its aim is to give an insight into certain parts of this beautiful area and to suggest how you may make the most of a day's outing. It includes details of nearby attractions, picnic spots, tourist information centres and car parking.

There are helpful suggestions for accommodation and places to obtain food. Nowadays most village pubs provide food, but unfortunately not so many places cater for children. Moreover many attractions confine their opening hours to the main season, being shut in the winter. Opening hours are included in this book but do check to avoid disappointment.

It helps if you can use a map and have the *Ordnance Survey 1:50,000 White Peak Map*, or the *Dark Peak* map for the northern part of the region. These maps show every field, lane and footpath which means that

The National Park symbol is the millstone

with a little practice you can extend your outing without being an expert on maps.

The western side of the Peak District receives far less visitors than most of the area. We included a walk in this area and also a bike ride in the Manifold Valley. It was a lovely sunny day in midweek and we chose to ride from Waterhouses, although you can do so equally well from Hartington village. We covered 10 miles and hardly met a dozen people all afternoon. So, despite the popularity of some areas, one can visit them in midweek and find peace and quiet as we did.

We hope the outings suggested here give you as much enjoyment as they have given us. We have had some really memorable outings and fond memories remain of good company and such wonderful scenery as there is in the Peak District — what more can one ask?

Graham Knight
Lindsey Porter

CHAPTER 1

Cromford
and High Peak Wharf

W hy Cromford? Most people just go straight
through here, heading for places like Crich or to
Matlock Bath where there are many visitors about at a
weekend. Cromford is one of those places where it pays
to stop and look around. It is perhaps understandable
that people tend to go straight through on the A6
because the village is set off the main road.

It was completely different about 200 years ago
because the road through the village by the Greyhound
Hotel to the Via Gellia and towards Wirksworth was a
market place. Cromford grew as a result of Sir Richard
Arkwright's cotton spinning textile business which he
established here. He was the originator of a new
technique in cotton spinning and his mill, built in
1771, was the world's first water-powered cotton
spinning mill.

His reasons for choosing this area were principally
that he needed water power and also security for his
new invention. Additionally he wanted a higher social
status than he had achieved in Nottingham. He became the squire of his own village and virtually everything here was initially built by him. The **Greyhound
Hotel** was built because he needed somewhere for
customers to stay. He provided a market and built a
quadrangle of shops, one or two of which have survived
including what is now a video shop to the right hand
side of the Greyhound Hotel. There was need for a
blacksmith and so that too was provided and survived

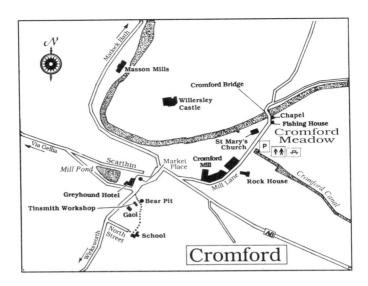

Cromford

opposite the hotel for nearly 200 years. It is now a shop but has kept the connection in its name.

The walk around Cromford village starts opposite the road junction with the **Via Gellia** road. Proceed up the alleyway or 'jennel', rounding a corner to where there is quite a deep water course on the left, and where the Tinsmith Workshop now exists. There are two sources of water coming in to a rather deep round stone-lined pit known as the Bear Pit. The deeper water course is part of **Cromford sough** (pronounced 'suff') a lead mine drainage channel, dating from 1673. The sough provided an unbroken flow of water. A further supply drains into the pit from the mill pond located behind the Greyhound Hotel. Both water courses have been channelled off towards the A6 and Arkwright's original mill. It crossed Mill Lane on a cast iron aqueduct, built in 1821. The second mill at Cromford was built within about a decade of the first.

Behind the adjacent **Tinsmith Workshop** there is a little courtyard containing the old village jail. The lock up is now owned by the Arkwright Society. It is situated to the right hand side of two black garage doors and if you look through the window you can see the two cells at the rear of the room. Retrace your steps to the Bear Pit and turn to the right. The path continues past an old pigsty and behind various buildings eventually reaching a school at the end of North Street. It passes the rear of a long line of houses in North Street. Just below the roof you can see where a row of windows have been infilled with stone. This is where looms would have been kept for the tenants who worked in this building, doing 'out work' for the mill. Reaching North Street, on the left is the school built in 1832. There is a tremendous amount of character in this wide, split level street with its stone built cottages. At the northern end is the Bell Inn, formerly the Blue Bell Inn. The cottage on the opposite side was also a pub originally called the Greyhound Inn. From North Street, take the Via Gellia road to the delightful mill

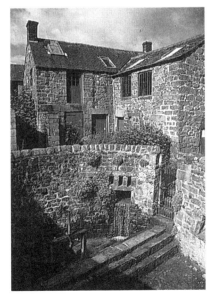

Cromford sough

pond. At the far end is a cast iron waterwheel at what used to be an old paint grinding mill. Locally mined iron-ore was ground up here to provide pigments. Wicker baskets are now imported from around the world for resale here. Another well known example of a paint grinding mill was Milldale Mill in Dovedale by Viator Bridge.

Behind the mill turn into **Scarthin**, which soon gives a splendid view of the mill pond. Arkwright had several dams created behind this, up in the Via Gellia, to ensure an adequate supply of water. Today it makes an interesting walk from the Greyhound Hotel up the main road to the water wheel and back along Scarthin. Standing above the mill pond is a useful place to stop and take in a wider vista. If one looks skyward above the sign of the Greyhound Hotel you can see a building just below three trees that stick out over the sky line. This is one of the old engine houses on the Cromford and High Peak Railway and a walk along the trail from the High Peak Wharf on the Cromford Canal is recommended later. The trail takes you up to that building and on to Black Rocks which are also visible at the right hand end of the skyline.

Upon returning to the Greyhound Hotel, cross the A6 into **Mill Lane** and under a green painted aqueduct of iron construction dated 1821. The Arkwright Society now occupies the mill buildings and various information boards give a good insight into their use. A wander around the site is recommended and there is a convenient coffee shop here too. Outside the mill, in Mill Lane, water not required for the mill wheels ran along the side of the road to the Cromford Canal and past the mill manager's house. Above is **Rock House**, Arkwright's home. It was his intention to move from here to Willersley Castle across the River Derwent. You can see the drive to the house beyond Cromford Bridge. When Arkwright was alive it was being rebuilt unfortunately he died a year before it was finished.

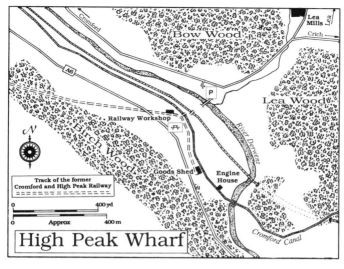

High Peak Wharf

The **Cromford Canal** is well worth exploring. The
wharf buildings were occupied for over 200 years by
Nathaniel Wheatcroft and Son Ltd as wharfingers. The
company was succeeded by the Cromford Canal Society
who operated a horse drawn narrow boat passenger
service from the wharf. The buildings contained a
visitor's centre highlighting the history of the canal.
Unfortunately this facility has now closed.

Just beyond the canal is **St Mary's Church** which
Arkwright had built on the site of an old lead smelting
mill. Arkwright's body was later moved from Matlock
and is now buried here. Cromford Bridge is on the old
road from Cromford to Matlock. The present A6 road
through Matlock Bath was not constructed until the
nineteenth century and for centuries before that,
indeed probably from Roman times when there would
have been a ford here, the road to Matlock climbed up
the hill past Riber and dropped down into Matlock.
Just before the bridge there is a square shaped building with the legend *Piscatoribus Sacrum*. It is an old

fishing house built in similar style to the fishing house in Beresford Dale which was constructed by Charles Cotton. Of more interest are the adjacent remains of a little medieval bridge chapel. It remained here in ruins without its roof and was eventually dismantled in the last century after the church was built. It is a shame it was pulled down after having survived for so long but there are sufficient ruins still standing to give a reasonable idea of what it looked like. Close by the remains of the chapel on the bridge parapet there is an inscription recording the fact that a man was coming over the bridge in 1697 when his horse leapt right over the parapet and into the river some 20ft below. Another thing which is not immediately obvious is that this bridge has been widened and the arches on the north side are completely different in shape to those on the other side.

The tour ends here. However it may be extended by walking along the canal towpath from Cromford Wharf to High Peak Junction at the wharf that existed at the side of the canal with Cromford and High Peak Railway. If you do not have sufficient time you can always drive over Cromford Bridge for just under $1\frac{1}{2}$ miles. There is a car park called **High Peak Junction** at the side of the road. After leaving your car, cross over the river and the railway to find yourself standing between the sewage works and the canal, with the old railway buildings beyond. This is a whole new area for you to explore and a fascinating little backwater.

There is a lot to be seen at the High Peak Junction especially if the workshop buildings are open. Inside is the oldest insitu railway line in the world. It dates from between 1825 and 1826 when the line was opened as a horse-drawn tramway. It was later turned into a railway and these are the original workshops. The original fish bellied rails marked with the initials of the **Cromford and High Peak Railway** can be seen by the maintenance pit. The old line climbs very steeply from here under the A6 and up towards Black Rocks. This was the only railway line in the country that was built to connect two canals and the original intention was to put a canal right across the Peak District. However the problems with water, locks and tunnels was so great that they decided a 33 mile horse-drawn tramway was a better solution. It had several fascinating statistics including the tightest curve anywhere on British railways and the steepest incline on any British railway worked by a locomotive without being pulled up by cable. A lot of the buildings up on the plateau had no water and so water tankers filled up daily here. The water column and tank survives adjacent to the large pulley which carried the cable at the bottom of the incline.

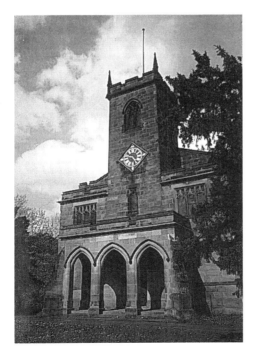

St Mary's Church at Cromford

You can walk up the **High Peak Trail**, it is signposted to Black Rocks which is $1^{1}/_{4}$ miles away, or go on even further to **Middleton Top** where one of the old steam engines complete with all its machinery, boilers and chimney survives as a museum. You can also have a picnic here and hire a bicycle too. Middleton Top is about $2^{1}/_{2}$ miles away and of course considerably higher in altitude. If you want just a short stroll why not go down the side of the canal. It is a site of scientific interest and some of it forms part of a nature reserve, so please do not pick or touch anything. Just look and while you are on your way you will pass the wharf buildings where the canal boats were loaded and unloaded. Eventually you come to the Wigwell Aqueduct over the River Derwent and you can see an engine house here containing a beam pumping engine dating from 1840. This was erected to bring more water to the canal from the River Derwent following alterations to the Cromford sough. This old engine house is open on certain days and the huge engine is steamed. A visit is recommended.

16

P **Car Parks**
On the streets in Cromford village and by the canal wharf in Mill Lane.

Picnic Areas
Canal wharf at Cromford and High Peak Wharf.

Places to Eat
Cromford village and Cromford Mill have tea rooms.

Toilets
Cromford village and rear of Cromford Canal Wharf.

Recommended Attractions

Cromford Mill
Mill Lane
☎ (0629) 824297
Open: 9.30am-5pm weekdays. 10am-5pm at
weekends. Visitors enquiries and shop.

Heights of Abraham
Matlock Bath (adjacent to railway station)
☎ (0629) 582365
Open: Easter to end October daily, 10am-6pm (later in
high season). A cable car to the Tree Tops Visitor
Centre, two show caves (old lead mines) and the Victoria Prospect Tower.

High Peak Junction Workshops
High Peak Junction, near Cromford
☎ (0629 82) 2831
Open: Easter to October, weekends. June, July and
August, everyday 10.30am-5pm.
Railway workshops of Cromford and High Peak Railway. Displays, video, model working forge, shop.

High Peak Trail
Former railway line and Cromford Canal towpath.
Linear walkways in quiet countryside.

Lea Gardens
Lea, Matlock
☎ (0629) 534380
Open: mid-March to end July, daily 10am-7pm.
The woodland setting for over 500 different rhododendrons. Well recommended in the spring.

Middleton Top Winding Engine House
Middleton Top, Wirksworth. Signposted off the B5036
Cromford to Wirksworth road. ☎ (0629) 823204

Open: Easter to October, 10.30am-5pm, Sundays (engine static); first Saturday in month and Bank Holidays (engine operating). Restored beam engines built in 1829 by the Butterley Company to haul waggons up a 1:8 $^3/_4$ incline on the Cromford and High Peak Railway.

National Tramway Museum
Crich, near Matlock
☎ (077 385) 2565
Open: late March to October, weekends and Bank Holidays, 10.30am-6.30pm; May to September, Monday to Thursday, 10am-5.30pm. Also some Fridays. Over forty restored trams in a Victorian setting. Enjoy a $1^1/_2$ mile tram ride. Ideal in the wet.

Peak District Lead Mining Museum
The Pavilion, Matlock Bath
☎ (0629) 583834

*Open: daily except Christmas Day 11am-4pm (later closing in summer). A fascinating reminder of the ancient lead mining industry. The **tourist information centre** is next to the museum.*

John Smedley Ltd *(Factory Shop)*
Lea Mills, Matlock
☎ (0629) 534571
Open: Monday to Saturday 10am-4pm. Knitted goods available. The Smedleys purchased the factory from the family of Florence Nightingale, who lived at Lea.

Whistlestop Countryside Centre
(Derbyshire Wildlife Trust)
Old Railway Station, Matlock Bath
☎ (0629) 580958
Open: Easter to end of October every day, 10am-5pm, winter weekends only 12noon-4pm.
Shop and free exhibition on local wildlife.

CHAPTER 2

Roystone Grange
Archaeological Trail

T his outing commences at Minninglow Wharf car
park, which is adjacent to the bridge over the road
from Parwich to Pikehall. The car park is on the site of
Minninglow railway station on the Cromford and High
Peak Railway. The latter was built to connect two
canals and so the stations were called wharfs, as on a
canal. The railway line is now a trail (the High Peak
Trail) for ramblers and cyclists. It crosses the Derbyshire plateau giving marvellous views, peace and quiet
and havens for flora and fauna.

The **Roystone Grange Archaeological Trail** (4
miles in length) is a circular path taking in part of the
High Peak Trail and then part of a drover's road before
taking to the fields. The drove road originally went to
Wirksworth and can be traced from Cheshire, cutting
just north of Leek near to The Roaches. Having crossed
the moors it came through Hartington and Biggin and
across the plateau and onwards towards Wirksworth
and presumably Derby. The old road, now a green
road, is soon left and a path heads down towards
Roystone Grange Farm. A lot of granges in this area
have connections with monasteries in medieval times,
and this was no exception. Unfortunately, the properties that were built at that time no longer survive and
archaeological work here has uncovered the foundations of the old grange which the monks used in the
twelfth and thirteenth centuries. In addition the
remarkable find of an old Roman farm can also be

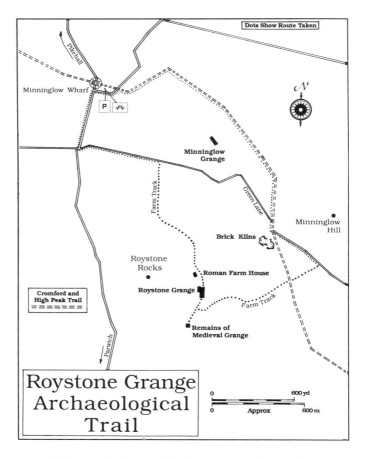

Dots Show Route Taken

Pikehall

Minninglow Wharf

P

N

Minninglow
Grange

Farm Track

Green Lane

Minninglow
Hill

Brick Kilns

Royston
Rocks

Roman Farm House

Cromford and
High Peak Trail

Roystone Grange

Farm Track

Parwich

Remains of
Medieval Grange

Roystone Grange Archaeological Trail

0   600 yd

0   Approx   600 m

seen. This particular walk allows you to investigate
evidence of farming stretching back 2,000 years.

From **Minninglow Wharf** car park the trail runs
eastwards, away from the road. The trail is flat and
soon reaches Minninglow embankment, faced with
stone and worth more than just a passing glance.
Ahead on the skyline is an isolated clump of trees
known as **Minninglow**. It is the site of a prehistoric
burial mound known as a cyst. It consisted of slabs of

stone forming a chamber and with another big slab forming a roof to it. Inside were interred the remains of prehistoric settlers of this area. There are a lot of these lows or tumuli in this area. They include Arbor Low, a large stone circle with Gib Hill adjacent to it which is perhaps the largest tumuli in Derbyshire. Just to the north of that is the Benty Grange tumuli at Parsley Hay. This is very well known in archaeological circles because the remains of a helmet of a Saxon Christian warrior were found here.

The line passes an old quarry where the remains of an old crane can be seen together with old railway lines in the quarry siding and a short length of a narrower gauge tramway laid to bring stone from the face to the railway. The trail leaves the quarry to cross over another large embankment perhaps 50ft in height.

Leaving the embankment, look for the old **lime kiln** on the left hand side. Here limestone was burnt to create lime to spread on the fields. It was fed in at the

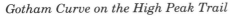

Gotham Curve on the High Peak Trail

top with coal, sealed and left for several days. The lime was then extracted from the bottom. Just beyond the lime kiln two gates are reached. This is where the trail is crossed by the drover's road and the route bears to the left. However if you climb up onto the right hand of the track you can see the remains of a circular wall. It is part of a nineteenth-century brick works that existed on this site. Not too much is known about its history or even its output. However it is typical of the many works which were built adjacent to the railway, including Friden Brickworks which survives at Newhaven.

The drover's road leads away from the railway as a broad grassy track between high dry-stone walls. Upon reaching the third field on the right, look for the stile. Once over the wall, cross the field heading for the archway beneath the railway line. Emerging from underneath the line, the fields slope down the valley towards **Roystone Grange Farm**. Upon reaching the left hand side of the farm, turn left and head for the building in the valley bottom. An interpretation board on the building advises that it was an old engine house to a pump which sent air to the rock drills used in the quarry passed at the side of the railway. Of more interest perhaps is the site of the remains of the old medieval grange that was established in the reign of Henry II and then extended in the thirteenth and fourteenth centuries. As the illustration on the notice board shows, it was at one stage possible to see all the foundations of the building but now it has all been back-filled and only the main outside walls can still be seen. Fields of Roman origin have also been located nearby and details of these are also given on the notice board.

Returning to the farm, proceed past the house to the last building where another interpretation board awaits. It is adjacent to the Roman farm house that existed here. The sign indicates that a house platform was discovered here and excavation revealed an aisled

Medieval ruins at Royston Grange during excavation

Roman villa. It had low walls and wooden vertical posts inside the stone wall that supported a tent type roof structure which was then covered with thatch. The remains of the house can also be seen.

From the farm, the track leads back towards another lane where you turn left. Turn right upon reaching the road from Parwich to walk a short distance to the old railway line and Minninglow Wharf car park.

 Accommodation
See under Hartington (page100).

 Car Park
At Minninglow Wharf on the Pike Hall to Parwich road.

 Picnic Areas
Minninglow Wharf and other former stations on the High Peak and Tissington Trails including Friden and Hartington. Also near Elton: from Minninglow take the road north under the railway bridge to Pikehall. Turn right

and take the Winster road at a fork. Then take the second turn to the left.

Places to Eat
Hartington and numerous local pubs such as The Blue Bell Inn near Tissington and The George Inn, Alstonfield. Carriages Restaurant, Newhaven.

Toilets
Hartington and Tissington Stations on the Tissington Trail and in Hartington village.

Recommended Attractions

Gotham Curve
Upon reaching Minninglow Wharf car park, turn left and walk about half a mile to what used to be the tightest curve on British railways. The line turns through 80°.

Hartington Village
Very popular village with souvenir shops, but also other necessities including a petrol station, grocers, doctor's surgery and plenty of accommodation. It also has two factory shops selling cheese (including Hartington Stilton), and terracotta pottery.

Parwich
Small uncommercialised village nearby. The adjacent hamlet of Alsop-en-le-Dale has a small church with Norman features.

CHAPTER 3

Swainsley and Ecton Hill

T he Manifold Valley is justifiably popular with many visitors to the Peak District. However, the majority only know it from its roads. More discerning visitors know the value of the many footpaths which surround and cross the valley. Some give memorable views down into the valley and across to Morridge and the Warslow Moors or eastwards into the limestone plateau area of the White Peak. The paths are easy to follow and once away from the valley itself, the noise of the crowds fade and are replaced with a serenity one never forgets.

This outing begins at **Swainsley Tunnel** in the Manifold Valley, which may be reached by taking the valley road from Hulme End, on the B5054 Warslow to Hartington road. Turn by the Manifold Valley Hotel towards Alstonfield and then take the first turn to the right. Having passed the right turn to Warslow and the old copper mine tips at Ecton, the road crosses the River Manifold at Swainsley. A turn to the right just beyond the bridge brings you to the tunnel where a car may be parked either near the tunnel or on the right, across the old railway bridge over the Warslow Brook. Retracing ones steps over the road bridge, there is a gated road on the right. This route to Wetton Mill has more or less been superseded by the old railway track and it is rare to find a car on it. It therefore makes a useful path, avoiding the motorised Swainsley-Wetton Mill section of the old railway line.

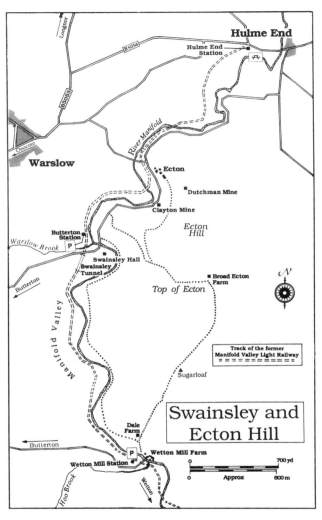

Soon, **Swainsley Hall** comes into view across the valley. It was built in 1867 and modified early in the twentieth century. It has an enviable setting in this lovely section of the valley. Leaving the hall behind,

Refreshments are available while visiting Wetton Mill

one passes a dovecote in the grounds of the house, complete with birds! The old road contours around the hillside. It is now a far cry from the days when long packhorse teams laden with copper ore passed this way from the Ecton mines, heading for Wetton Mill, Grindon Moor and eventually the smelting works at Whiston, near Froghall in the Churnet Valley. The entrance to one of the mines is opposite Swainsley Hall. It is an early nineteenth-century test digging or trial and should not be entered. It contains much water and nothing of interest. It is not advisable to go exploring such excavations.

The road eventually reaches **Dale Farm** at **Wetton Mill**. Here you turn right to find Wetton Mill Farm and a tea room where you can pause for a rest. There is little to see of the old corn mill which was originally on the site. The waterwheel, when it existed, was somewhere near the present site of the farm dairy. The mill existed in 1617 and was here possibly as early as 1577, but it had closed by the mid-nineteenth century.

Here there is a choice of routes. Either return up the

valley to Swainsley on either side of the river or take a
more energetic option by leaving the valley for the
climb up onto **Ecton Hill**. The path passes through the
Dale Farm yard. Ahead is a large outcrop of reef
limestone — a fossilised coral reef. The path rises up
the left hand side of it and then bears to the right
towards a stile. Another stile gives access to the field
on your left. The path runs alongside the field wall for
a couple of fields and then continues on the other side
of the same wall to reach a paved road in front of
Broad Ecton Farm. Mine workings from the Manifold Valley at Ecton reached this farm in the 1880s —
the sound of blasting below could be heard above
ground. The entrance of this mine (known as the
Clayton Mine) is by the roadside at Ecton. Water is
still seen issuing from it.

From Broad Ecton Farm, the path turns to the left,
running up the left hand side of the wall for the first
two fields. It then cuts diagonally across the next field
before heading towards the top of the valley side and a
stile in the wall. From **Broad Ecton**, there are distant
views across the Peak and southwards too, but the
most memorable of the views occurs when one reaches
the top of the valley. Down in the valley sits Swainsley
Hall, the river curling around it, the whole scene
wrapped in a medley of green fields and woodland. The
valley of the Warslow Brook leads the eye away and
over the moors to the treeless expanse of **Morridge**.
The latter merges into Axe Edge and the vista returns
towards the valley, with Warslow and Longnor villages
clearly visible.

Again a choice of routes presents itself, depending
upon the amount of time available. A path drops
quickly down into the valley, heading for Ecton Lea,
the cottages to the north of the tunnel. On the Ordnance Survey map *'Outdoor Leisure — The White
Peak'*, the cottages are referred to as, 'The Lee' and the
road bridge here as 'Ecton Bridge'. Its true name is

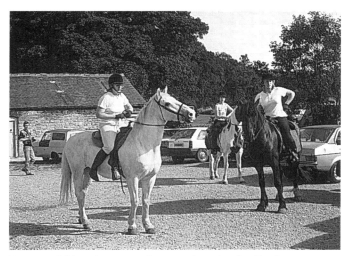
Pony trekking is a popular pastime in the Peak

Stamps Bridge, after the former nearby stamps mill or
crushing mill which ground down copper ore.

The route involves a fairly steep descent — whether
to Ecton Lea or alternatively to Ecton and strong
walking shoes or walking boots are recommended.
From the stile turn to the right and walk northwards
before dropping down on a distinct path to Ecton and
the house with a copper spire. Just beyond the house
the path reaches the valley floor and a return to one's
car along the old **Manifold Valley Light Railway**
track. This alternative path gives an extension to the
memorable view and a good impression of the layout of
the old mine. However much of the waste limestone
rock has been removed and the tips were formerly
much larger.

P **Car Parks**
Swainsley Tunnel and Wetton Mill
(on site of old railway stations).

Picnic Areas
Wetton Mill. Picnic tables also at Hartington
Station and Hulme End Station.

Places to Eat
Wetton Mill tea room, pubs in adjacent
villages (Alstonfield, Butterton, Warslow and
Hulme End) and Hartington.

Toilets
Wetton Mill (tearoom patrons), Hartington.

Tourist Information Centre
Hartington Railway Station
Open: Easter to September, Saturday, Sunday
and Bank Holiday Mondays.

Recommended Attractions

Hartington Village
On the B5054

*This well known and very popular village has a number
of shops. There is a bank (National Westminster, open
Friday only), filling station, gift shops, cafés, hotel, post
office and the stilton cheese factory shop. In Beresford
Dale, south of the village, Charles Cotton's fishing
house, built in 1674 may be glimpsed through the trees,
across the River Dove.*

Manifold Valley Light Railway
*Some of the railway buildings survive at Hulme End,
but the engines and picturesque coaches have all been
scrapped. The 8-mile long track-bed from Hulme End to
Waterhouses is now a tarmac-covered footpath / road;
there is a short tunnel at Swainsley. Some stretches are
ideal for the disabled, although the gates on certain
sections may preclude a wheelchair.*

Manifold Arts & Craft Centre, Butterton
*Craft Centre, licensed restaurant, camping & bed &
breakfast ☎ (0538) 304320*

CHAPTER 4

Cycling in the Manifold Valley

T wo of the most beautiful of the Peak District valleys are the Manifold Valley and the Hamps Valley; or at least the limestone section of each. In 1904 the Manifold Valley Light Railway opened and ran through the two valleys until 1934. The line was converted into a footpath and until recently cycling was banned on its tarmac surface. This has now changed and cycling along the old railway line is becoming increasingly popular. Visitors to the valley at a week-end could be forgiven for thinking that it is always as busy.

Bikes may be hired on the site of the old railway station at **Waterhouses**. Take the road at the side of the Crown Inn, go under the bridge and turn left. The Cycle Hire Centre is in the old goods shed. The old railway ran down the Hamps Valley to Beeston Tor. It is slightly down hill, a feature lost on a rambler, but noticeable on a bicycle. Roughly midway, the line passes **Sparrowlea**. There used to be a railway station here but now this has gone. There is an adjacent farm used as a tea room. The next station was at **Beeston Tor** where the Hamps Valley meets the Manifold Valley. The old railway refreshment room — provided by a local farmer — still survives close to the confluence of the two rivers.

One of the delights of this outing is the abundance of flowers in the areas flanking the line. There are over 200 species recorded in the valley. From Beeston Tor,

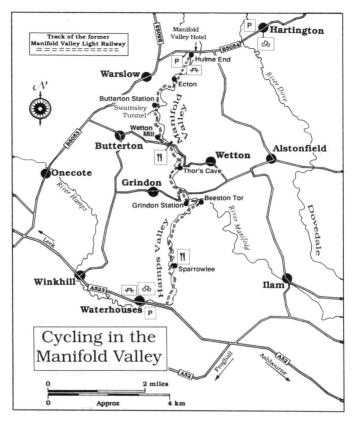

Cycling in the Manifold Valley

the line ran up to Hulme End. Near to Beeston Tor, the old packhorse road from Grindon to Alstonfield crosses the valley. Here was Grindon Station close to Weag's Bridge. The ride is now uphill, but no hardship, as it passes through the most dramatic section of the valley below **Thor's Cave**. This huge cavern mouth belies the absence of a cave system beyond it. Many people climbing up the path from the river to the cave must be disappointed by this, although the view should compensate. If you do make the climb, it is worth knowing that the cave entrance is often slippery, in wet weather particularly. It is no place to lose your footing.

Below the cave is a useful spot to rest a while — there are many such places in this delightful valley. About a mile or so further on is **Wetton Mill** with its well known tea room. Many people who have booked their bike for 3 hours pedal this far, with a stop for refreshments and then return. If you hire your bike for longer (or bring your own) you may continue on from here towards Hulme End, 3 miles further up the valley. Wetton Mill is 5 miles from Waterhouses.

Continuing on there is a choice of routes. The railway track is used by motor traffic from just below Wetton Mill to Swainsley Tunnel. If you prefer to avoid this, the old road between Wetton Mill and Swainsley offers an alternative route. Stay on the tea room side of the

The views are rewarding from Thor's Cave

river until a T-junction is reached below Swainsley Hall. Turn left, over the bridge and bear to the right to rejoin the old railway at the tunnel. The road is not as flat as the old line but the lack of traffic, including fewer ramblers and cyclists, is an advantage.

From Swainsley, the track passes the old copper mine tips at **Ecton**. Here copper was mined that sheathed East Indiamen and admiralty ships and went into much of the country's brass during the eighteenth century. It also provided the money used to build The Crescent at Buxton. The railway arrived too late for mining operations, but a cheese factory was established here which did use the line, sending milk to London each day. At **Hulme End** the old ticket office and carriage shed survives 67 years after the line closed. Their survival is due to their use as a highway depot, although ideally the buildings would be better served as an interpretation centre for the old railway. Upon reaching the main road, proceed (or dismount and walk) to the old Light Railway Hotel, now the **Manifold Valley Hotel**. You can take lunch here before returning back down the valley.

A 16 mile trip may sound arduous but it is not. This description has been chiefly of the line itself. However, the scenery and flowers to be seen on route make this a memorable outing, one to be recalled with pleasure long after the visit.

Picnic Areas
Wetton Mill, Waterhouses and Hulme End.

Places to Eat
Other than the tea rooms mentioned, many local pubs offer food. Alstonfield and Butterton pubs are especially recommended. In Waterhouses there is a high class restaurant (The Old Beams) and a chip shop. There are several restaurants and tea rooms in Hartington. The Yew Tree Inn at Cauldon Low is an old village inn noted for its

good ale and antiques. To reach it turn up the road by the Crown Inn in Waterhouses.

Toilets
Waterhouses cycle hire centre and Wetton Mill (for tea room patrons only) and Hartington.

Tourist Information Centre
Hartington Railway Station
No telephone number
Open: Easter to September, Saturday, Sunday and Bank Holiday Mondays.

Recommended Attractions

At The Waterhouses End
Coombes Valley Nature Reserve
Six Oaks Farm, near Apesford, Leek, Staffs
Open: Tuesday, Thursday and weekends.

Moorland Farm Park
Ipstones Edge
Follow signs from Bottom House on the Leek to Ashbourne road (A523). Ideal for young children.

At Hulme End
This route can be cycled in the reverse direction, hiring a bike in Hartington.
A.J. & M. Sears
Market Place, Hartington, Buxton
☎ (029 884) 459
Open: daily, except during January and February then weekends only.
This involves an extra $2^1/_2$ miles each way but there is much to see in Hartington. See chapter 11.

CHAPTER 5

The Churnet Valley

T his outing starts at **Belmont Pools** situated on
the road to Cheddleton from Ipstones in the south-
west corner of the Peak District. It is a little area very
well known to people from Stoke-on-Trent, but even
they used to refer to the Churnet Valley as the 'Hidden
Valley'. It is a beautiful, tranquil place with a canal
and a little-used railway, plus a few cottages and the
Black Lion Inn at **Consall Forge**. The road to the
latter used to be privately owned and therefore access
was denied to everybody except those on foot or on the
canal or railway. Today it is possible to reach the pub
by car if you drive beyond the recently opened nature
centre. This is reached from Consall village which is
near Wetley Rocks, south of Leek.

The start of the path is easily reached from Ipstones.
Take the road to Cheddleton (Belmont Road) and park
close to the largest pool's dam once Belmont Pools are
reached. The path commences at the east end of
Chapel House Farm which you will have passed at
the road side. It was originally built as a religious
building when the owner of the Belmont Estate fell out
with the local vicar in Ipstones. He built this little
chapel with its east window and small tower for him-
self. After the two men were reconciled it fell into
secular use. It is now a dwelling house — notice the
date over the door (1794). From here a path descends
into the wood, crosses a stream and then climbs to a
flight of steps to join the drive to **Belmont Hall**. This

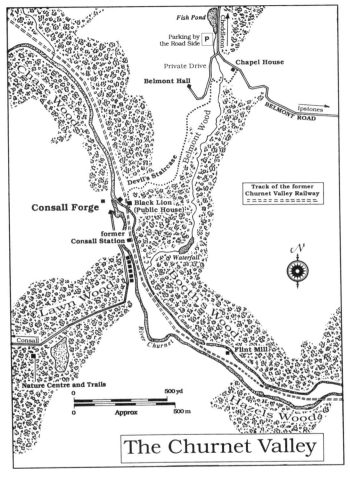

is followed a few yards before leaving the drive as indicated by a sign. The hall (which is private and so not open to the public) was one of the homes of the Sneyd family. They had various seats around here including Ashcombe Hall, Woodlands, Belmont and Basford Halls. Belmont Estate was sold off in 1917.

Having left the drive the path skirts the top of the wood, following yellow arrows to the top of what is called the **Devil's Staircase**. This is an exceedingly long flight of steps which takes you down to Consall Forge. The path follows a wall separating the field from the wood. The steps should be descended — there are 199 of them!

The path from the bottom step soon leads to the rear of the **Black Lion Inn**. Ahead are the **Caldon Canal** and railway. The latter was built across part of the canal and the railway station had to be cantilevered out over the canal. If you walk southwards you can see the restricted width of the canal and the railway waiting room. This is the only piece of the cantilevered section which still survives. About half an hour's walk from the Black Lion Inn brings you to the former **flint mill**, a water powered mill where flint was ground for the pottery industry. Here there is a winding hole where narrow boats can turn around and a lock.

The canal divides in front of the pub. Upstream from here, the River Churnet and canal are combined but at

The Black Lion Inn at Consall Forge

Consall Forge they are separated again. This accounts for the floodgate across the canal by the arched bridge in front of the pub — it stopped flood water entering the canal. A seventeenth-century iron forge stood on the land between the canal and the river just below where they separate.

Beyond the canal it is possible to see a large battery of stone built lime kilns, similar to those further down the valley at Froghall. It is recommended that you allow time for a wander along the towpath. The pub makes a useful stop for refreshments. You can leave here by the road route to climb out of the valley and up to the nature centre.

Until recently it was possible to travel by a horse-drawn passenger narrow boat from Froghall to the flint mill. It was a very tranquil way of exploring the valley. Now one has to be content with the towpath walk. Once you have explored enough, retrace your steps up the Devil's Staircase and back to Belmont Pools.

If you want to make a circular walk, continue down the canal past the flint mill in the direction of Froghall.

Cherry Eye Bridge on the Caldon Canal

Just after a mile or so beyond the Black Lion Inn, you reach the small stone-built **Cherry Eye Bridge**. A path climbs northwards from here to Booth's Hall Farm and then crosses the field to Belmont Road. Turn left here to follow the road back to your car.

 For the Disabled
Access to Consall Forge may be obtained via the canal towpath from Cheddleton, or by car from Consall.

 Picnic Areas
Froghall Wharf and Oakamoor (former copper works site).

 Toilets
Leek, Waterhouses (old railway station site) and Froghall Canal Wharf.

Recommended Attractions

Alton Towers Leisure Park
Alton, North Staffordshire
☎ (0538) 702200
Open: major rides and attractions, mid-March to early November daily 10am-5, 6 or 7pm depending on season. Grounds and gardens: all year round 9am-1 hour after attractions close, with much reduced admission rate in winter. Europe's premier leisure park with over 120 rides and attractions, free once entrance fee has been paid. Theme areas and magnificent gardens, on former estate of the Earls of Shrewsbury. Over fifty catering outlets, free parking, facilities for the disabled.

Cheddleton Flint Mill
Cheddleton, on the A520, south of Leek
Former flint mill with two waterwheels. Situated adjacent to the Caldon Canal with a preserved narrow boat Vienna. *Mill operates every weekend.*

Cheddleton Railway Station
Cheddleton, on the A520, south of Leek
Station preserved with memorabilia of the North
Staffordshire Railway, including rolling stock.
For further information ☎ (0782) 411411.

Consall Nature Park
Situated at Wildacres, near Consall village on the road
to Consall Forge.
Woodland walks.
☎ (0785) 223121 ext 7265

Moorland Farm Park
Ipstones Edge
Follow signs from Bottom House on the Leek to
Ashbourne road (A523). Ideal for young children.
Open: daily 10.30am-dusk April to November.
Admission charged.

RSPB Coombes Valley Nature Reserve
Situated near Bradnop on the Leek to Ashbourne road
(A523)
Follow signpost 'RSPB Coombes Valley Reserve'.
Open: Tuesday, Thursday and weekends
☎ (0538) 384017.

CHAPTER 6

Gradbach

West of the A53 Buxton-Leek road lies the village of **Flash**, close to the boundary of Staffordshire with Derbyshire and Cheshire. From Flash, the road runs downhill to Gradbach and Allgreave. Just before reaching the River Dane, amid the trees lies Manor Farm and a little lane to Gradbach Mill Youth Hostel.

This lane runs down the side of a brook before climbing the hillside to the large gateposts that mark the drive to the youth hostel, housed in a former silk mill. Leave the car in the car park at the bottom of the hill and walk up the hill and down the drive to the mill. A path is clearly marked from here proceeding downstream past the former mill house. It emerges from the fields at Caster's Bridge over the Black Brook where it is possible to cross the stream and enter **Back Forest**. From here there is an option of continuing down to Danebridge. The path continues diagonally up the hillside and past the remains of a very small cottage. It was demolished in the 1950s and was known as **Furnace Bottom**. What a delightful, if isolated, position it occupied! The path rises steeply 50 or 60ft uphill from the brook to join a rather wide path. The climb then becomes much more of a gradual incline heading for Lud Church. Over to your right, across the valley by the side of the road you will see a grey painted cottage. It has three windows upstairs that enables you to easily identify it. Called **The Eagle and Child** it used to be a pub although it is now just a tea

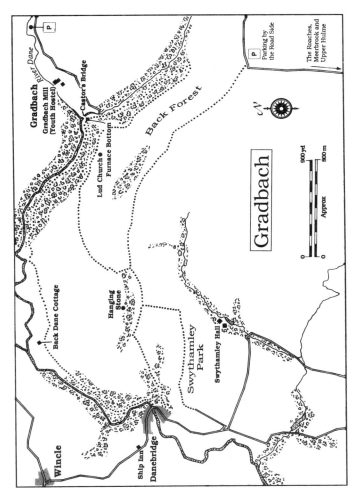

room. It stands on an old packhorse route from the silk
mill at Gradbach which went over to Wildboarclough.
There is a plaque dated 1783 on the building showing
an eagle carrying a child away. Just inside the porch
there is also a plaster motif of an eagle carrying away a

child. The building is a reminder of the industries which existed in this area. It was built on this meeting of two packhorse ways at a time of plentiful silk production, and it was also on a main Cheshire packhorse way which came up this valley towards the Peak District via the Three Shires Head. The pub got its name from the Stanley family crest as the eagle and child feature on their coat of arms. The Stanley family are the Lords Derby who have a large estate just north of Liverpool and have a country seat in the next valley at Crag Hall in Wildboarclough.

The path eventually levels off and there are some rocks to the right which are a useful marker. Here there is another little path which goes off sharply to the left almost going on itself. There is a little stone sign marked **Lud Church** at ground level which directs you along this narrow path. The path runs parallel but above the one that you have just left, going back in the direction just walked. After 200 to 300yd look for a path to the right into a cleft in the rock. This is the entrance to Lud Church. It is a landslip, about 60ft high about 10ft wide or so and 200ft long. The path drops down a set of stone steps to get into the chasm. Upon turning a corner the full impression of the landslip is revealed and it is an amazing sight, despite the curve which prevents you seeing all of it at one time. It is called Lud Church because it was used by religious dissenters in the fifteenth century known as the Luddites. It had nothing to do with the early nineteenth-century rioters who smashed textile machinery, although some writers tend to confuse the two. It is said that the congregation was found here by soldiers and during the discovery a girl called Alice de Ludauk was killed. Years ago there used to be a wooden statue of Alice high up on the rocks midway down the cleft. Old photographs of Lud Church often show this statue. Before leaving, compare the two sides of the cleft. One side is just rock with a green mould

Gradbach Mill has now been renovated to become one of the Peaks youth hostels

upon its surface but the other side has grown lush with mosses, ferns and even an occasional tree clinging to the edge.

Walking back to the main path, there is a choice of retracing your route or continuing to Danebridge. Either way it is worth stopping to admire the views. Bear in mind that you are in Staffordshire; across the river is Cheshire and some of the hills at the head of the Dane Valley are in Derbyshire!

As one walks towards Danebridge, the high ridge drops suddenly to the flat Cheshire plain. This escarpment is known as **Bosley Cloud** which features in an interesting custom that happens in Leek. In midsummer, people congregate at the back of the old parish church on the 20, 21 and 22 June for the sunset. If the conditions are right, with no haze on the horizon, you can see the sun set down behind Bosley Cloud. It then reappears again at the side of the hill and proceeds to set again across the plain so you can see the sun set completely twice.

Continuing onwards from Lud Church, the path is virtually level. It proceeds over the ridge and then drops down towards the valley which opens out on the side of the Swythamley estate. You pass a renovated farm cottage and then the track bears down to the left where there is a sign for **Back Dane Cottage**. Wander down the lane here and turn right when it reaches a large stone wall at the Swythamley Hall grounds. This lane brings you to the road to Danebridge. Turn right and walk down to the hamlet with its huge bridge spanning the river.

If time and energy permits, a detour from the sign for Back Dane Cottage may be made. Above and to the right is a large outcrop of gritstone rock called the **Hanging Stone**. The view is better from here, and there are two plaques on it worth reading for yourself. One is a memorial to Lieutenant Colonel Courtney Brocklehurst of Swythamley who died in Burma in 1942. He was the man who established a zoo on The Roaches; the other plaque is to a former squire's dog. Once in **Danebridge** you can cross the bridge and climb up on the road a little way and take refreshments in the Ship Inn if you wish. Until recently it had some interesting relics of the 1745 rebellion. However one of the landlords despatched them off to London for auction. They included a newspaper from Macclesfield which one of the Scottish Jacobean soldiers carried, together with his flintlock.

To return to Gradbach, take the stile at the bridge and then walk up the side of the river through the river meadows and skirting the moor. The footpath is well marked all the way back to Gradbach, eventually reaching the bottom section of the Back Forest. If you have got the time (or indeed on another occasion) it is worth stopping off at Danebridge and taking the path downstream from the Wincle side of the bridge. The footpath goes down through a trout farm and cuts through delightful scenery across the river meadows.

Eventually it comes out at **Gig Hall Bridge** which is a foot bridge across the river at a place where the feeder for the **Rudyard Reservoir** begins. The reservoir was built to provide the Caldon Canal with water and so the feeder itself looks just like a canal with a towpath at the side of it, except that it was not built for navigation. Your walk may be extended down the feeder if you prefer. Either way this path makes a lovely diversion, especially on a summer afternoon. There are more concessionary paths around Back Forest; look out for a map of them on notice boards. All are easy to follow.

 Accommodation
Gradbach Mill Youth Hostel
Gradbach Mill
Gradbach
Quarnford, Buxton
☎ (0260) 227625

 Picnic Areas

Meerbrook: by Tittesworth Reservoir. There is an impressive childrens' play area here with a café and plenty of picnic tables. Facilities extend to a summer barbecue and information centre. Macclesfield Forest Visitor Centre has picnic tables by Trentabank Reservoir but no café.

Places to Eat
The New Inn, Flash; The Ship Inn, Swythamley; Meerbrook, by Tittesworth Reservoir; The Eagle and Child tea room, on the Allgreave-Gradbach road.

 Toilets
Meerbrook, by Tittesworth Reservoir.

 Tourist Information Centre
Macclesfield
Town Hall, Market Place
☎ (0625) 21955

Recommended Attractions

Brindley Water Mill
Mill Street, Leek, Staffs
☎ (0538) 384195
Open: Easter to end of October, weekends and Bank
Holiday Mondays 2-5pm; July and August also Mon-
day, Tuesday and Wednesday 2-5pm.
Operational cornmill. Museum of the life and times of
James Brindley (engineer) 1716-1772.

Macclesfield Forest Visitor Centre
Situated adjacent to Trentabank and Ridgegate Reservoirs. There are woodland trails and a heronry here.
For further information contact the tourist information
centre at Macclesfield.

Macclesfield Silk Museum
Heritage Centre, Roe Street, Macclesfield
☎ (0625) 613210
Open: Tuesday to Saturday 11am-5pm, Sunday 2-5pm.
Closed Mondays (except Bank Holidays), New Year's
Day, Good Friday, Christmas Day and Boxing Day.
Admission fee charged.
Winner of the 'Come to Britain' 1987 Special Award.
First museum in Britain to be devoted entirely to the
study of the silk industry. Award winning audio-visual
programme. Costume, textiles, room settings, scale
models, museum shop, tea room.

Pavilion Gardens
Buxton
☎ (0298) 78662
Large area of parkland plus The Pavilion (refreshments), conservatory, swimming pool and childrens'
play area.

Rudyard Lake
Situated off the Leek-Macclesfield road (A523).
Circular walk around the lake.

The Roaches
Large outcrop of rock off Leek-Buxton road (A53) with
ridge walk and splendid views.

The bridge at Quarnford near Gradbach

CHAPTER 7

Three Shires Head

High on the moors of Axe Edge between Buxton and Leek, lies the headwaters of the River Dane. It is an area of little streams, moorland, rugged farms and countless packhorse routes now preserved as footpaths. The White Peak map in the Ordnance Survey Outdoor Leisure series is invaluable. It is possible to link up various old packhorse routes to make walks of varying length and interest. Above all, the area of the upper Dane Valley seems to offer an appeal hard to find elsewhere in the Peak. Its composition of woodland, moor and pasture comes together as an unforgettable experience for many people, a feeling that is hard to define.

To explore a little of it, proceed from Buxton or Leek to **Flash Bar** (named after the old toll bar) and the Traveller's Rest Inn. On the Buxton side of the inn is a lane to **Knotbury**. There is no village as such, just a hamlet of scattered farms. Follow this lane — it drops gradually downhill to the second T-junction. Park on the grass verge in this area — wherever seems convenient but not across a field gate! Walk up the road to the right which leads to Readyleech Green Farm. Bear left here, through the gate. At the end of the field on the left, the lane bears to the right and a path drops downhill directly ahead. It cuts the corner and leads down into **Blackclough** on a little lane above a small brook. Look out for the alum spring on your right; its deposits now spread out and cover the stone wall by

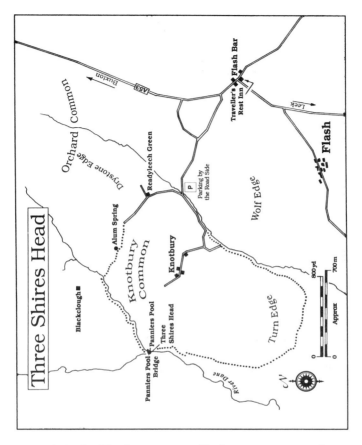

Three Shires Head

the roadside. The lane eventually becomes unpaved
and follows the valley bottom down to the Dane Valley.
Here is a marvellous packhorse bridge known appro-
priately as **Panniers Pool Bridge**. Take a look under
the bridge arch. It has clearly been widened at some
stage. Several packhorse routes converged upon this
bridge, connecting Cheshire with the Peak District.
Despite a shortage of place name evidence, some of
these tracks must have been saltways, carrying salt

traffic into the Peak and coal away from the moorland pits at Axe Edge which existed here.

Standing on the bridge, tracks may be seen on either side of River Dane as one looks downstream. At **Panniers Pool**, just below the bridge, Staffordshire meets Derbyshire and Cheshire. Our path is on the east or left side of the river and in Staffordshire. The sandy path gradually climbs up the valley side, the views improving as one climbs higher. The path starts to curve away from the River Dane, extending the view down to Gradbach and Back Forest.

The track becomes paved again after a while and follows another stream between Turn Edge on the left and Wolf Edge on the right. This quiet lane eventually leads back to your car.

This is such a beautiful place to visit on sunny summer days and it is worth making an effort to reach it. If the walk cannot for some reason be undertaken, take your car from Buxton up the Macclesfield road. Bear off the A52 a mile or so before reaching the Cat and Fiddle Inn onto the Congleton road. After 2 miles, there is a paved road off to the left which connects with Gradbach. Take this lane. After a short distance, it reaches **Cut-Thorn Farm**, below the road on the right hand side. An unmade track leads off to the left opposite the farm. The car must be left here and parking is not easy. However, the track is only half a mile from Panniers Pool Bridge. It is not ideal for wheelchairs, but adventurous minded people may like to try it.

There are few facilities in this Moorland area, but refreshments and toilets are available locally at three of the highest inns in England. The New Inn at Flash, the Traveller's Rest Inn at Flash Bar and the Cat and Fiddle Inn on the A537 Buxton-Macclesfield road. The Cat and Fiddle is the second highest inn in England at 1,690ft. There is a visitor centre with refreshments facilities at Tittesworth Reservoir.

CHAPTER 8

Lathkill Dale

O ne of the most beautiful valleys, or dales in the
Peak is Lathkill Dale. This outing covers perhaps
the most interesting section, with an option to continue
if you prefer a longer walk. It starts conveniently at the
car park in **Over Haddon** which is signposted off the
Bakewell-Monyash road (B5055). Having parked the
car, walk down the hill to **Lathkill Lodge** and turn up
river. Go carefully because this section is a National
Nature Reserve. Be particularly sensitive about wan-
dering off the path, picking flowers or generally dis-
turbing the flora and fauna, walls, fences, etc. A
permit, which is not freely available, is required if you
want to wander off the footpath. For further information contact the Nature Conservancy Council,
Riverdale House, Dale Road North, Darley Dale
☎ Matlock 734343. It is not a public footpath as a sign
near Lathkill Lodge explains. There is plenty to see in
the valley including trees, flowers and fish in the
crystal clear water of the River Lathkill. Additionally
there are the remains of lead mining and the valley
once had one of the largest water wheels in England.

At the start of the walk there are leaflets which you
can buy. They are left in pouches at the side of the
footpath. You are on trust to pay a small fee; they are
worth it and are quite informative, giving a very good
insight into the valley and how it has developed over
the centuries. The orientation of the valley (which runs
west to east) has meant that one side receives more

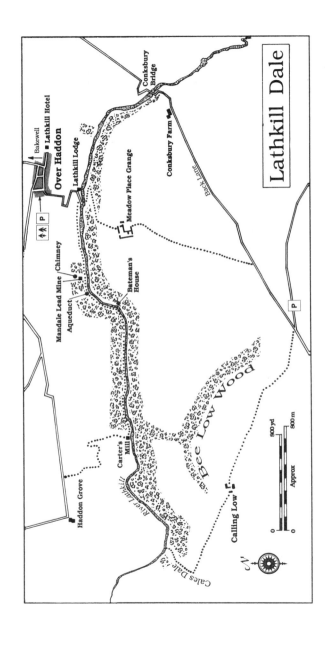

Lathkill Dale

sunshine than the other. This has produced different kinds of soils. Consequently different kinds of plants grow on each side of the valley creating environments of great diversity. On the right hand or north side the plants are much smaller as a result of grazing and thinner soils. By comparison, on the left hand side the ground is wetter and moist and the plants and herbs are much taller. There are fewer plant species on that side because everything is so much bigger and there is less room for the small ones to develop. This in turn has created different habitats for insects. Of particular interest at the Monyash end of the valley is the largest habitat in the country of a flower called Jacobs Ladder. The footpath goes right through the middle of this large bed and the flowers are fenced off. Signs indicate what they are and why they need protection. You are encouraged to look and learn without picking. It is an offence to interfere with them in any way. As you proceed up the river, look for the fenced off hillside on the right. This is done to permit sheep grazing, which keeps the grass short. In turn, this allows smaller, rosette type plants to grow which otherwise would soon disappear.

Upon reaching the woodland you find a large drainage channel from the **Mandale lead mine**. Even if it appears dry, remember it is dangerous to enter. It is possible to follow an earth track to the right between some sycamore trees to reach the mine itself. All that remains is what is called the bob wall. The large engine housed here consisted of a cylinder with a huge cast iron beam which sat on the top of the bob wall. To the rear of it is a shaft where the pumps sat and where the water was drawn from the depths of the mine out into the drainage level. Details of the mine can be obtained in one of the above mentioned leaflets. There also used to be a waterwheel here. This was also used for pumping, the more expensive coal burning engine was used as a last resort. The water channel or 'leat' for the waterwheel ran for quite a way up the valley and crossed it on an aqueduct.

Retrace your steps to the valley path and continue up river. This valley shares the beauty of Dovedale although it lacks the pinnacles of Dovedale. The stream is delightful; the water is crystal clear and it is easy to observe the fish. The wooded nature of the dale is a sheer delight. Passing the aqueduct piers and crossing a meadow, the ruins of a house can be seen from across the river. This is **Bateman's House**. It was built for a Mr Bateman who had designed a new kind of pumping engine. It was installed in a shaft situated within the house and built in this manner so that no one else could steal the idea of the engine. It is all fenced off now because the house is in ruins and the shaft exposed. The southern side of the valley is private ground and it is emphasised that you need a permit to gain access. On no account should you enter this area without one. Additionally, dogs and children should be kept out of the river however tempting it appears. The river is an important element of the nature reserve.

Eventually the path leaves the wood and with it the character of the dale changes. Just before this the path passes a pond with a weir which once provided the water for Mandale mine. Upon leaving the wood there is another weir that was constructed to provide water for **Carter's Mill**. The mill was still operating during World War II but now it has gone almost completely. You can still see the grindstones of course because they were too big to remove. Unfortunately everything else has virtually disappeared without trace except for the weir which still provides a picturesque pool of water on its up stream side. Try and bring bird-watching and flower-spotting books with you because the flora and birdlife are particularly rich in this valley.

You may retrace your steps from here or make a circular walk. You may turn right at Carter's Mill and head for Haddon Grove Farm. From there, return by

Enjoy an afternoons walking along the beautiful Lathkill Dale

lanes to Over Haddon. Alternatively continue upstream and cross the river after half a mile or so into Cales Dale. From here, head for Calling Low Farm, the car park at Long Rake and then Meadow Place Grange. The path is waymarked but the O.S. White Peak map is recommended.

Picnic Area
Long Rake, off the Bakewell-Friden road, west of Youlgreave.

Places to Eat
Over Haddon has a tea room in the main street.
Lathkill Hotel at Over Haddon offers good food
and a superb view over the dale.
There are various places in Bakewell.

 Toilets
Over Haddon, Bakewell and Youlgreave.

Recommended Attractions

Bakewell
*This is the only town in the National Park and the
National Park Headquarters can be found here. The
church is particularly worth visiting, plus the Old
House Museum behind the church.
For further information see page 78.*

For further information see page 78.

58

Haddon Hall
*Bakewell
☎ (0629) 812855
Open: late March to beginning October daily except
Mondays (and Sundays in July and August) 11am-
6pm. Unspoilt medieval and Tudor manor house with
magnificent terraced rose garden, set in the beautiful
valley of the River Wye.*

Monyash
*Old lead mining village, retaining its
uncommercialised appearance. Still retains one of its
four meres or village ponds. A footpath runs down the
length of Lathkill Dale from Monyash. The section
mentioned above is only a small part of it. Ideally you
need two cars, one in Monyash and the other in Alport,
near Youlgreave. Alternatively use the Ordnance Survey
'Outdoor Leisure' map for The White Peak. With this
you can plan a circular walk to suit your walking
requirements.*

Over Haddon Craft Centre
Situated in a converted barn at the east end of the main village street.

Youlgreave
Small village to south of Lathkill Dale above the banks of Bradford Dale, a tributary of the River Lathkill and particularly beautiful.

The remnants of Mandale Mine

CHAPTER 9

Chatsworth

T his outing begins in **Edensor** village as it is part of the history of Chatsworth. It also enables you to savour the view of the big house while walking through the park and over the River Derwent into the grounds. The present village was founded after the demolition of the original village, done so that it would not impair the Duke of Devonshire's view from Chatsworth House. The first half of the village was removed to what is now Pilsley and at a later date the Duke decided that the rest should go. The traditional story is that the architect who drew up the plans gave the Duke a book full of different ideas. The Duke could not decide which to take for the basis of his village. He therefore had one of each style. Whether the story is true or not, the houses are certainly all of different design! The village is worth looking at and do not forget the **church** too.

If you want refreshments here visit the post office tea room. It is situated between the church and main road. The churchyard contains the grave of John F. Kennedy's sister. The late American President came to Chatsworth to visit his sister's grave. Lord Frederick Cavendish was also buried here after his murder in Phoenix Park, Dublin in the 1840s. The posy of flowers sent by Queen Victoria is still in the church. From Edensor cross the road and walk on the very distinct path opposite and over the brow of a hill to look at Chatsworth House itself. The path passes a little cottage with no road to it and completely surrounded

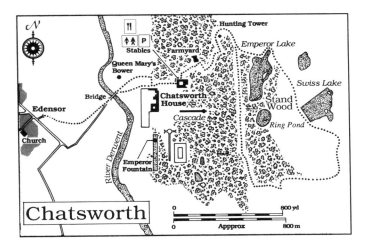

Chatsworth

by a wall. The former village used to be situated here.
The cottage used to front on the old high street which
has now grassed over. When it was planned to move
the village the occupant of this cottage refused to leave.
The Duke relented and the house still survives. Possibly, the reason for the Duke's change of heart was
because the cottage was hidden by the brow of the hill
and so could not be seen from Chatsworth.

Chatsworth is incredibly popular and it is encourag-
ing to see that by and large people treat the park with
respect. Upon reaching a brow the path drops towards
the River Derwent and suddenly you can see the house
in its splendour and beauty. It is sometimes difficult to
comprehend that everything you are looking at was
planned. Its natural look was deliberately set out this
way by Capability Brown (one of Britain's most famous
gardeners). He was so successful that very few traces of
the first Duke's formal garden which had been set out
here survive. The Cascades seen at the back of the
house date from the first Duke's time as does the
Hunting Lodge on the skyline. The maturity of the
trees that can be seen here came many years after

Capability Brown's death. It shows what forethought he had, and the degree of professionalism that he brought to the construction of gardens and parkland around a country house.

The bridge over the river is a convenient place to stop and look around. Just to the right of the house there is the huge plume of water from the **Emperor Fountain**. When it was built it was the largest gravity fed fountain anywhere in the world although now it does not often get to its full height. The water is fed from the Emperor Lake at the top of the hill behind the house, which will be visited later in the walk. The fountain was constructed in 1844 for a proposed visit to Chatsworth by Tzar Nicholas of Russia. He was a friend of the Duke but in the event he did not come and so he never saw it. Eleven years later the Tzar sent a Russian log cabin to Chatsworth. Not many people know where it is situated. Looking to the right and downstream from the bridge you can see the hills climbing away covered with trees. Nestling against the southern edge of that wood is the **Russian Cottage**, as it is known. It can be seen from a footpath but unfortunately no paths pass directly in front of it.

Looking back to the front of the main house it is worth remembering that the house built here by Bess of Hardwick still survives. Only the outside of the building has been changed. The basic internal structure built by her remains. The gardens were re-laid from their Elizabethan design by the fourth and sixth Dukes. On the northern side of the bridge is another Elizabethan survivor called **Queen Mary's Bower**. Mary Queen of Scots was a prisoner here and it is said that this little enclosure with the steps up to it is where the Scottish queen used to walk and take a little fresh air. High on the skyline of Stand Wood is the **Hunting Tower**. This also dates from the period when Bess of Hardwick lived here. The walk takes you to this tower and then across the flat area and around the lakes beyond it and finally back down into the park again. From the bridge, continue up to the **farmyard** and **adventure playground**. Having crossed over the cattle grid the road forks. It is straight on for the farmyard and adventure playground and right for

The historic Chatsworth house lies in some of the Peak's most picturesque countryside

Chatsworth stages many events throughout the year

Stand Wood. Just as you leave the farmyard the road bears round to the right to reach a large group of cut stone on your right. Immediately to your left there is a little track which takes you up to a road. Turn to the left and then bear right on a track into **Stand Wood**. The path starts to climb up the side of a little brook and up a long flight of steps on to the **Hunting Tower**. It is four storeys in height, commands a marvellous view across the valley and is a convenient place to stop and rest. From the Hunting Tower the footpath proceeds to the rear of the tower and then after a few yards turns to the right. Walk along this stretch of woodland path and look out for mauve painted signs directing the route. You eventually reach a large lake on the right hand side known as the **Emperor Lake**. This is the one which provides water to the Emperor Fountain.

Continuing along the track it reaches the **Swiss Lake** on the left hand side after about a quarter of a mile. You can continue from here around through the wood to emerge at a spot where you can turn left and leave Stand Wood altogether. Alternatively, continue on bearing round to the right returning to the Emperor Lake and back to the Hunting Tower where you drop back down into the park again. This is a short walk of about $2\frac{1}{2}$ miles, since there is so much else to see and do. It pays to come early and make the most of the time available. There is the house and the garden to be viewed, either together or separately. In addition you can walk freely in the park on the west side of the River Derwent. There is also the garden centre down at the **Calton Lees** end of the estate where you can get a pleasant snack as well as have a browse around a centre with everything from plants to paintings. The nearby stables now incorporate a café with reminders of the horses which formerly were housed there. To complete the attractions offered by the estate is the farm shop at **Pilsley** with its associated craft shops.

Perhaps one of the best times to come is when you know the bluebells are in flower. The woodland around the lakes is then a beautiful blue carpet with a distinctive fragrance. Also at that time of year the rhododendron and azalea are out in the house garden. A little later in the season it is worth visiting the huge laburnum tunnel. You can easily spend a full day around Chatsworth and its estate and who can ask for anything better, particularly during the early summer and in the midweek when hopefully you will find it less crowded.

Places to Eat
Additional to Chatsworth are various surrounding pubs, Caudwell's Mill and The Cavendish Hotel at Baslow although the latter is expensive.

Toilets
Chatsworth House car park; Baslow.

Recommended Attractions

Caudwell's Mill and Craft Centre
Rowsley
☎ (0629) 734374 (mill) or 733185 (craft centre)
Open: October to March, daily 10am-4pm (weekends only in January and February).
   Historic water-powered flour mill, café, gift and craft shop, working crafts including wood turner, glass blower, potter and clock-makers. Wholemeal flour always available.

Chatsworth Estate Farm Shop
Stud Farm, Pilsley, near Bakewell
$1^1/_2$ miles from Chatsworth House
☎ (0246) 88392
Open: Monday to Saturday, 9am-5.30pm all year

round. Fine selection of fresh meats, vegetables and ready prepared foods, including game from the estate in the season. Range of craft shops.

Chatsworth House
Bakewell
☎ *(0246) 882204*
Open: April to end October (dates may vary a little), daily 11.30am-4.30pm. Historic house and garden. Farming and forestry exhibition and adventure playground, open end March to end September, 10.30am-5.30pm.

There is a family admission to the farmyard and adventure playground. For the price of two adults and one child, up to three more children go in free. No dogs (but dog pound provided).

Haddon Hall
Bakewell
☎ *(0629) 812855*
Open: late March to beginning October daily except Mondays (and Sundays in July and August) 11am-6pm.

Totally unspoilt medieval and Tudor manor house with magnificent terraced rose garden, set in the beautiful valley of the River Wye.

CHAPTER 10

Longshaw Lodge and Padley Gorge

L ongshaw Lodge is situated close to the A6011 on the road between the Fox House Inn and Grindleford. It dates from about 1830 and was owned by the Duke of Rutland. The sixth Duke lavished a considerable amount of money to create one of the best sporting estates in the country. Across the estate 20 miles of drives were laid out. The estate was broken up in 1927 when 11,500 acres of land were sold. Some 750 acres, including the lodge, were acquired and presented to the National Trust. Today the Trust owns some 1,600 acres. The lodge is let privately as flats, but there is an information centre adjacent to it with a shop and cafeteria. This is open throughout the year but only at weekends in the winter months.

The estate has a car park at the rear of the lodge. It is situated just to the south of the Fox House Inn on the B6054 road to Froggatt. Whether you approach on the A625 from Sheffield or Hathersage, or on the B6521 from Grindleford, upon reaching the inn take the B6054 for 250yd and the car park is on your right. There is an information board here giving some details about the estate. If you can, pick up the National Trust leaflet called *Walks On Longshaw*. It has a most useful map of the Trust's estate.

Upon reaching the lodge turn to the right and walk up the drive and across the B6521. Walk through the wood and take the path that bears to the left to cross the **Burbage Brook** on a small wooden bridge. A well

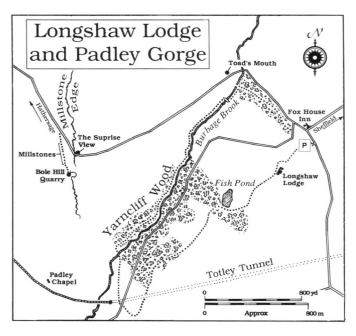

Longshaw Lodge and Padley Gorge

Toad's Mouth

Millstone Edge

Hathersage

Burbage Brook

Fox House Inn

Sheffield

The Suprise View

Millstones

Bole Hill Quarry

Yarncliff Wood

Fish Pond

Longshaw Lodge

Padley Chapel

Totley Tunnel

0   800 yd

0   Approx   800 m

marked path follows the brook. This is a very popular
area and ideal for a picnic by the side of the stream.
Just before the path reaches Padley Wood, look out for
the millstones scattered amongst the rocks. They were
obviously cut in-situ from large rocks lying on the
surface.

The path follows the brook down through **Padley
Wood**, high above the water which flows through
massive rocks. When the water level is high enough,
there are often quite dramatic views of rushing white
water. Padley Wood is a delightful area in itself. It is
one of the few areas where the ancient woodland cover
still survives, with sessile oaks, many birds (including
the wood warbler and the pied wagtail) and an abundance of woodland flowers. The path eventually leads
down to the brook which should be crossed and reaches

*Higger Tor
from
Carl Wark*

*Burbage
Brook in
Padley Gorge*

the road above the portal to the railway tunnel above Grindleford station.

Cross the road and take the path that rises up through the wood. It is a steep climb, but not too long! Upon reaching the top of the wood, turn left and follow the path with the wood on your left and fields on the right. At the end of the last field, one climbs a stile and heads across towards the large pond in **Longshaw Meadow** in front of Longshaw Lodge. Turn right at the pond and head up to the lodge. The meadow is the site of England's oldest sheepdog trials. They are held every September and were established in 1898. If you want a much shorter walk, there are plenty in the grounds of the lodge itself.

A trip to this area should also include a short walk to **Bole Hill Quarry**. Take the A625 towards Hathersage. The road goes around a sharp right hand bend known as **The Surprise View** — because of the magnificent view down into the Derwent Valley. A further 250yd down the road or so, park and take the path marked by a National Trust sign 'Bole Hill'.

The path is broad and flat, although descending down to the quarry. It is an old railway line which eventually descended to the river by a steep incline. After about 200yd look out for the abandoned mill-stones. Initially there are a few on the right and then 200 or so on your left, stacked against each other in several rows. Beyond here the path enters the wood-land area of the reclaimed quarry. Look out for the many ant hills in the wood. They are built of twigs and leaves and can be over 6in high. There are so many that they completely preclude the idea of a picnic in this lovely area.

Places to Eat
Longshaw Information Centre, the Fox House Inn and the Grouse Inn (on the B6054).

Recommended Attractions

Carl Wark Hill Fort
Due north of the Fox House Inn. Iron Age hill fort in an impressive position.

Padley Chapel
Part of the now demolished Padley Hall. The Fitzherbert family who owned the house were Roman Catholics. In 1588, when the faith was prohibited, two priests were arrested here and hanged in Derby. The building probably dates from the fifteenth century. The rest of the house was demolished in 1650. Take the road down to Grindleford Station and follow the unmade track beyond the station.

The Derwent Edges
High above the east side of the River Derwent, the top of the valley is a series of gritstone edges. A footpath runs along much of the escarpment and is very popular with ramblers. The view stretches for miles.

A Word About The National Trust
The National Trust, along with the Peak District National Park, are the main agencies for the work of conservation in the Peak. Since 1975 the Trust has raised over £1 million to be used in its Peak District Appeal. It has been used for instance to buy land to consolidate its estates, conserve and maintain buildings and habitats etc. If you are interested in this, it is worth obtaining the booklet *The National Trust in the Peak District: Conservation in Action.* Better still, join the Trust and make a donation to the Peak District Appeal. Help protect this beautiful countryside.

> The National Trust
> Clumber Park Stableyard
> Worksop
> Notts S80 3BE
> ☎ Worksop 486411

CHAPTER 11

Selected Towns and Villages

Ashbourne

Ashbourne was originally a small hamlet, probably situated near to its elegant church. However in the thirteenth century, the site of the town was moved to higher ground away from the river, leaving the church isolated and out of the town centre. It originally had a large triangular market place that had St John Street as its bottom side. Subsequent infilling has produced an area of interesting little alleyways including The Butchery.

Today there is much to see, both around the Market Place and in the surrounding streets where pavements throng with summer visitors. The properties fronting the north side of Church Street and the west side of the Market Place originally were planned with long narrow plots stretching to a lane at the rear — now Union Street. Several alleyways still connect with Union Street and provide convenient short cuts. Of particular interest is one of these called **Tiger Yard**, named after the former Tiger Inn. Building number 4 fronting The Butchery is Tudor and the original timber framing may be seen in Tiger Yard. Another timber framed building is **The Gingerbread Shop** in **St John Street** which has recently been renovated. This building dates from the fifteenth century. Further along is **The Green Dragon** shop, again timber framed and containing a salt cupboard bearing the date 1605.

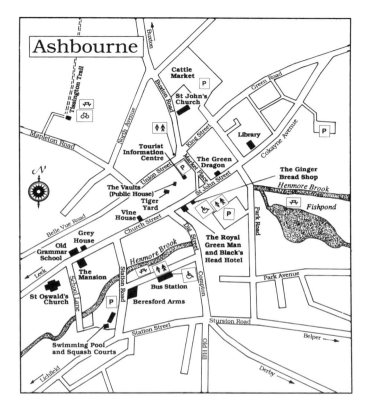

Of much later date, but no less interesting is **Peter
Cook's** chemists shop also in St John Street. Here the
Victorian shop front has been renovated most taste-
fully. Also in St John Street is **The Royal Green Man
and Black's Head Hotel** (known locally as The Green
Man), with its inn sign stretching across the street and
with a picturesque courtyard behind.

Ashbourne's main joy in its street scenes is **Church
Street** with its Georgian town houses. A small number
of shop fronts have been allowed to spoil some façades
but by and large the majority are untouched or blend
in well. From the centre of the town, one of the first to

notice is Vine House on the right, with its columned porch and vine! Also of interest here is the mullioned window of the cellar which clearly belongs to a previous house on this site. On the opposite side of the road are three houses grouped around a courtyard and built as almshouses for the widows of clergymen.

The adjacent house, complete with pilasters but with a modern shop front inserted, was built by a clergyman. It stands next to a very large property which was the town house of members of the Beresfords of Fenny Bentley. Beyond the disused railway tunnel, the Ivies can be seen on the right opposite two groups of seventeenth-century almshouses. Beyond here on the right is the Grey House which is stone faced to match the adjacent Old Grammar School. The **Grey House**, built in the mid-eighteenth century is a particularly pleasing building with a large Doric porch and Venetian windows. It is similar to the brick built Mansion opposite, a seventeenth-century building with a mid-eighteenth-century façade. Next to the Grey House is the **Old Grammar School**, founded in 1585 and now one of the school boarding houses.

At the end of Church Street is **St Oswalds Church** with its 212ft spire. The church dates from the thirteenth and fourteenth centuries, the east end being the oldest. It is a light church, and 176ft long. In the north transept are a group of monuments including the well known and poignant memorial to Penelope Boothby by Thomas Banks. This was Bank's most famous carving. It records the death of a little girl — an event which broke not only the marriage of her parents, but the health of her father. When exhibited at the Royal Academy exhibition, Queen Charlotte is supposed to have broken into tears. Also of interest in the opposite south transept is a brass plaque which records the dedication of the church in 1241. It is the oldest dated brass plaque in the country.

Ashbourne is of course famous for its Shrovetide

The timber-framed Gingerbread Shop is one of the oldest buildings in Ashbourne

football game. The ball is 'turned up' (thrown up) from the Shaw Croft car park after a lunch traditionally held at The Green Man. The game takes place on Shrove Tuesday and Ash Wednesday and played by the Up'ards and Down'ards through the streets, river and open country between the goals at Sturston and Clifton, which are 3 miles apart! Any walk around the town should include the park and fishpond east of the Shaw Croft car park and below the sad looking remnant of Ashbourne Hall. There is a river side walk here which is very pleasant in summer.

Railway enthusiasts will no doubt wish to seek out the old railway engine and goods shed of 1852 in

Clifton Road. Real ale enthusiasts may take more note of the Beresford Arms Hotel, formerly The Station Hotel. This was a tied house of James Eadie's brewery of Burton. His trade mark (a red cross) features in the stone doorway surrounds and in the stained glass above the entrances. This brewery was acquired by Bass in the 1930s.

Accommodation

There is plenty of accommodation available in the Ashbourne area and full details are available from the **Tourist Information Centre** in the Market Place ☎ (0335) 43666. It pays to book ahead even in the winter.

Car Parks

Parking is difficult in summer. If Shaw Croft car park is full (the one in the middle of town), seek out the free car parks at the cattle market (off King Street) and off Cockayne Avenue, beyond the park.

Cycle Hire

Mappleton Road, at the northern end of the railway tunnel on the Tissington Trail and at the School House in Tissington village.

Picnic Areas

There are picnic tables by the fishpond and against the River Henmore almost opposite the bus station and at the Tissington Trail cycle hire centre.

Places to Eat

There are numerous places in the town, but particularly good is Peter Cook's in St John Street. Several pubs offer food including The Green Man, The Vaults and the Beresford Arms (where you can park on the forecourt). The Ashbourne Lodge Hotel also provides bar meals

which are reasonably priced and caters for
vegetarians.

 Sports Facilities
A swimming pool and squash courts are on the
old railway station site in Ashbourne. Vehicular
access is from Church Street (adjacent to the
church). Tennis courts are adjacent to the car
park in Cockayne Avenue.

 Toilets
Top of the market place and bus station.

Recommended Attractions

Carsington Reservoir
*Situated south of Carsington and Hopton villages. It
was intended that water collection for this new reservoir
would begin in 1986 and a picnic area has already been
laid out. The dam wall collapsed in June 1984 and at
the time of writing the dam is being rebuilt. Rescue digs
in the area proposed to be flooded have revealed sub-
stantial Roman remains, which may be the site of*
Lutudarum, *the Roman's lead mining and smelting
centre in the Peak District.*

Fenny Bentley
*In the church is a curious tomb to Thomas Beresford
who fought at Agincourt. The effigies of both Thomas
and his wife are depicted bundled up in shrouds, as are
their twenty-one children around the tomb. The tower of
their fortified and moated manor house may be seen
from the A515 Ashbourne to Buxton road, or from the
footpath which passes close by. The church ceiling is
aluminium!*

Tissington Trail

The former site of Hartington railway station is now a picnic site with toilet facilities and an information centre in the old signal box. The latter still retains its old lever frames and there are several photographs on the wall showing what the railway used to look like. The trail gives level walking and cycling north from Ashbourne. Cycles may be hired from the National Park at Parsley Hay Wharf and Ashbourne. If you hire a cycle from Parsley Hay and end up in Hartington, return via Long Dale, as it is a much easier gradient. Proceed eastwards out of the village, past the school and take the first turn to the left, into Long Dale. Sections of this valley are part of the Derbyshire Dales National Nature Reserve.

Tissington Well Dressing

A visit to this village on, or just after Ascension Day, to see the annual well dressing ceremony should not be missed if at all possible. Using petals and other natural materials such as moss, pressed into clay set in a wooden frame, the five wells are 'dressed' to depict a particular religious theme. It is supposed to have originated as a thanksgiving for the ceaseless supply of pure water.

Bakewell

Set on the banks of the River Wye, Bakewell is an ancient and popular town in the heart of the Peak District that still retains its Monday cattle market. It developed as a crossing of the river, its bridge dating from 1300. Despite recent development in Bakewell, most of which has been outside the old town, it still retains considerable charm.

Overlooking the heart of the town is the church which stands on the hillside. The spire dominates the

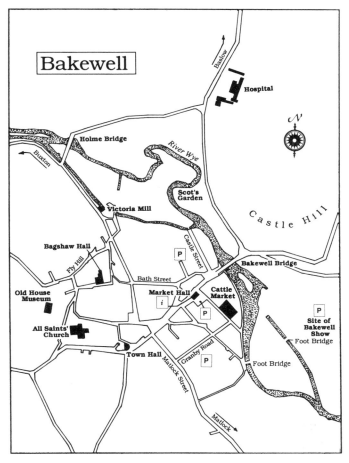

Bakewell

views across the town and dates from the nineteenth century. A visit to the **church** is worthwhile. It dates from Norman, possibly Saxon times and has several interesting features. The west front is Norman and two Norman arches survive in the wall between the nave and the south aisle. In fact the walls between the nave and the aisles may well have been the walls of the

'Saxon' church. However the latter was much extended in the thirteenth century. The structure deteriorated to the point that the spire, the octagon beneath it and the adjacent south transept had to be built in the nineteenth century.

During this rebuilding, many carved stones were recovered of Saxon and Norman age. Together they form the largest and most varied group of medieval monuments in the United Kingdom. They are stacked in the south porch and adjacent to the inside of the west font. On the hillside above the church is the **Old House Museum**. It was built as a parsonage house in 1543 and was turned into a tenement by Sir Richard Arkwright some 250 years later. In 1959 it was rescued from years of neglect by the Bakewell Historical Society. The church may be reached from King Street where another old and distinctive house may be seen. This is the old **Town Hall**, standing back from the road and with a large forecourt. It dates from 1602 and held a succession of different uses. The Town Hall

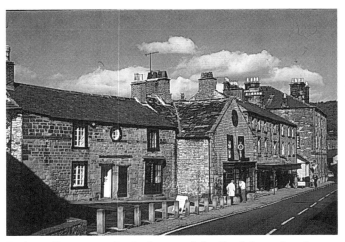

Bakewell is not only the heart of the Peak but also the home of the famous Bakewell Pudding

existed upstairs, with the St John's Hospital on the ground floor. In 1709 it was altered and almshouses were built behind it. Subsequent uses even included housing the town fire engine! Continuing up the street, the last house on the right is the original home of Lady Manner's School, established in 1636 in South Church Street.

North Church Street and Church Lane (to the north and west of the church respectively) come together adjacent to Bagshaw Hill which leads past **Bagshaw Hill.** It was built in 1684. In its kitchen garden was built the youth hostel, fronting onto Fly Hill. Bagshaw Hill leads down to Buxton Road (A6). Turning to the left here, the road passes the **Victoria Mill**, its huge waterwheel now resting in the millyard. Further up the road, past the fire station a path on the right leads to **Holme Bridge**. An interpretation board here describes the various watercourses built to serve Lumford and Victoria Mills. An old sheepwash can be seen beyond the sign.

The bridge is an old, narrow packhorse bridge, dating from 1664. It leads into Holme Lane. Opposite Burre House (about halfway down it from the bridge), there is a footpath through delightful river meadows known in part as **Scot's Garden**. It leads back to the main bridge and Bridge Street. Here one can walk back along the street and into the centre of the town again. Alternatively, the riverside walk can be taken below the bridge, but this time on the opposite, and west side of the river.

The centre of the town is **Rutland Square**. It was set out by the Duke of Rutland at the beginning of the nineteenth century, the Rutland Arms being built in 1804. Here, the famous accident occurred which gave us the Bakewell pudding. The contents of the pudding recipe were put in the reverse order and so the jam was at the bottom instead of the top.

Bakewell is as well known locally for its annual show

held in August. It used to be claimed that it was the largest one day show in Britain, but it now extends over two days. There are a significant number of interesting stands plus displays and competitions in its large ring. It is certainly well recommended, but allow a full day if you can.

P **Car Parks**
Adjacent to the Market Hall; off New Street and a large one by the cattle market. Also across the river on the showground site.

Picnic Areas
Adjacent to the River Wye.

Toilets
Adjacent to the Market Hall.

Tourist Information Centre
Bakewell
Old Market Hall
Bridge Street ☎ (062 981) 3337

Places to Eat
There are plenty of places to eat in the town and several pubs offer good food. A popular eating place is above Sinclair's china shop.

Recommended Attractions

Caudwell's Mill and Craft Centre
Rowsley
☎ (0629) 734374 (mill) or 733185 (craft centre)
Open: October to March, daily 10am-4pm (weekends only in January and February); March to October daily 10am-6pm. Historic water-powered flour mill, café, gift and craft shop, working crafts including wood turner, glass blower, potter and clock-makers. Wholemeal flour always available. Guided tours by arrangement in summer (including evenings).

Chatsworth House

Bakewell
☎ *(024 688) 2204*
*Open: April to end October (dates may vary), daily
11.30am-4.30pm.*
*Historic house and garden. Farming and forestry
exhibition and adventure playground, open end March
to end September, 10.30am-5.30pm.*
*There is a family admission to the farmyard and
adventure playground. For the price of two adults and
one child, up to three more children go in free.*
No dogs (but dog pound provided).

Haddon Hall

Bakewell
☎ *(0629 81) 2855*
*Open: late March to beginning October daily except
Mondays (and Sundays in July and August) 11am-
6pm. Totally unspoilt medieval and Tudor manor
house with magnifi-
cent terraced rose
garden, set in the
beautiful valley of
the River Wye.*

Haddon Hall

Monsal Trail
Pathway on former railway line from Chee Dale to Rowsley. Access from Station Road.

Old House Museum
Cunningham Place, off Church Lane, Bakewell
Open: Good Friday to end October daily, 2-5pm. Parties booked for morning or evening visits.
☎ (062 981) 3647
Folk Museum in historic early sixteenth-century house, once owned by Sir Richard Arkwright and partitioned to house some of his workpeople.

Buxton

The Romans realised the value of Buxton's thermal waters and for centuries their reputation has brought many people seeking a 'cure'. The fifth Duke of Devonshire recognised the need for facilities to cater for the growing number of visitors and presumably the profit that could be made. The Crescent which he built became a focal point for Georgian Buxton and it has remained so to this day. Today, Buxton offers more for the tourist than any other Peak District town and claims to be the highest town in England.

The Crescent was built as three hotels to accommodate visitors who had come 'to take the waters'. Today part of it houses the County Library and the remainder is currently empty. In October 1990 the buildings were featured in the *Daily Telegraph* as one of the top ten buildings at risk in the country. Not only is an occupier needed, but restoration work to the façade is also required. One has only to compare it with the work done on the library portion by the County Council. The fashion for hydrotherapy resulted in baths being developed either side of The Crescent. The south side

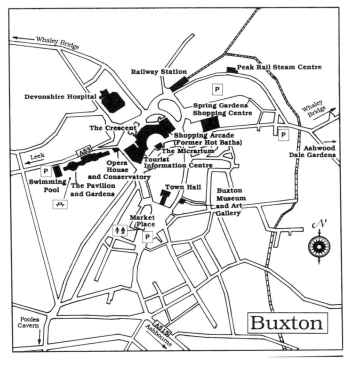

was for the poor, and now houses a Tourist Information Centre. The north side was occupied by the thermal baths with their warm waters. It is now an arcade of shops but retains the seat used for lowering people into the bath. The Pump Room opposite The Crescent used to be a centre for socialites who would sit drinking water brought up from the marble lined well at the rear of the building. Today it is used as **The Micrarium** — a centre for exploring the world beneath the microscope. However, it is still possible to see the well if you enquire.

Behind The Crescent are the former stables built by the Duke as facilities for guests staying at the Crescent's Hotels. The exercising area was later enclosed and the building converted into the **Devonshire Hospital**. The central dome used to be the world's largest unsupported dome. With its circular central area surrounded by its stone columns supporting the roof it is very impressive and worth a look. However please ensure you do not disturb patients or staff.

Nearby is the **Opera House**, adjacent to the Pavilion and its gardens. After years of neglect, the Opera House is enjoying a renaissance and is the centre for the popular Buxton International Arts Festival, now very much part of the national festival scene and held in July of each year. At the side of the Opera House is the **Conservatory** which is always well worth a visit. Beyond it there is a café at first floor level and a restaurant on the ground floor. Outside, the extensive gardens stretch away, incorporating a childrens' play area, miniature railway, a large lake and the town's swimming pool. It is justifiably a very popular area, immaculately kept by the District Council Parks Department.

Opposite The Crescent, the main road rises from the traffic lights towards Higher Buxton. Fronting this road is **Buxton Museum** which is well worth visiting.

The glass Pavilion and Pavilion Gardens at Buxton offer many attractions for all the family

In addition to its art gallery, it houses a large archaeological collection, including exhibits found in the caves of the Manifold Valley. It also has an impressive collection of Blue John stone ornaments and slices of the stone displaying its beautiful colours. There is also an intriguing re-creation of Professor W. Boyd-Dawkin's study together with his books and a table made of Ashford black marble. The professor was well known for his interest in the area's history, geology and archaeology.

Railway enthusiasts might have another Buxton museum nearer to their heart — the **Peak Rail's** rolling stock collection, kept adjacent to the British Rail station. The society aspires to bringing a railway service back again between Buxton and Matlock and the once 'impossible dream' is beginning to move towards reality. The new road past the station leads down to **Ashwood Dale Gardens**. There is a park here, either side of the infant River Wye, often overlooked by many visitors.

A recent and far sighted venture in Buxton has been the creation of a large shopping complex off **Spring Gardens**. It has a large arcade, allowing easy and comfortable shopping even in bad weather plus a large car park at the rear.

To the south of the town is the large **Buxton Country Park** which incorporates **Pooles Cavern**, the prettiest cave system open to the public in the Peak. The cave is relatively dry and flat, with many remarkable formations. There are several paths laid out in the park, including one which leads to **Solomon's Temple**. This position commands marvellous views across the Peak and is well worth the effort of walking up to it. To reach Pooles Cavern, take the road towards Ashbourne out of the Market Place. At the London Road traffic lights turn right and then follow signs marked for 'Pooles Cavern'.

P Car Parks
Opposite the railway station and also adjacent to the swimming pool in the Pavilion Gardens.

Picnic Area
At the Pavilion Gardens.

Places to Eat
Buxton is a good shopping area and there are numerous places offering refreshments and accommodation to suit all tastes.

Toilets
The market square.

Tourist Information Centre
The Crescent
Buxton
☎ (0298) 25106

Recommended Attractions

The Micrarium
The Crescent, Buxton
☎ (0298) 78662
Open: late March to end October, daily 10am-5pm.
Exhibition of nature beneath the microscope. Forty-four remote controlled microscopes projecting onto TV-sized screens.

Buxton Museum and Art Gallery
Terrace Road
☎ (0298) 4658
Open: Tuesday to Friday 9.30am-5.30pm, Saturday 9.30am-5.30pm. Extensive collections in geology, archaeology, prehistory and local history relating to the Peak District. Temporary art exhibitions monthly.

Pavilion Gardens
The Micrarium, The Crescent
Buxton
☎ *(0298) 78662*
Park, food, swimming, children's attractions.

Peak Rail Steam Centre
Buxton
☎ *(0298) 79898*
Steam Centre open: all year except Christmas and New Year, 10am-5pm.

Pooles Cavern and Buxton Country Park
Green Lane, Buxton
☎ *(0298) 6978*
Open: Easter to end October, daily, closed Wednesday (except high season) 10am-5pm.
Beautiful natural show cave; 100 acres of woodland with nature trail, free car park, picnic area, toilets, shop.

Castleton and Mam Tor

Perhaps the Peak's most popular village, it owes its origins to the former Royal Forest of the High Peak. This was an open area of forest and pasture affording sport to Norman kings. Here they built a fortified sporting lodge. Today, it survives largely intact as the only stone built castle in the Peak. Below it developed a small village around the church. Lead mining and agriculture seem to have been the mainstay of the local economy as the forest became settled. Blue John stone and the caves brought many tourists as early as the eighteenth century.

Today, the connection with Blue John stone is as strong as ever, despite dwindling reserves. Now the

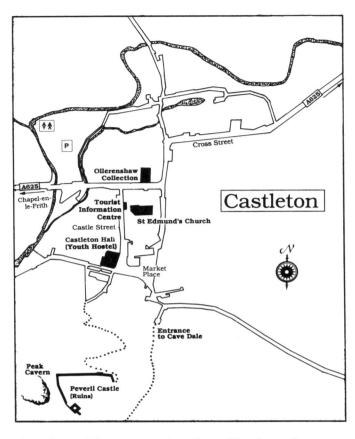

stone is used for costume jewellery. The days of manu-
facturing large ornaments, table tops, etc, have long
since passed. The heart of the village remains largely
intact, although modern development has spilled along
the main road through the village. The old properties
still surround the church and green, with the hall at its
northern side. The little lane at the left side of the hall
leads towards Peak Cavern.

St Edmund's Church has a Norman chancel arch
with a large zig-zag carved in it. A similar feature can

be seen in the remains of the entrance arch to **Peveril Castle**. Parts of the castle date from the eleventh century. From surviving records the keep can be dated to 1176 and remains largely intact, except for the original wooden external staircase. Facing the village there is a curtain wall which dates from the eleventh century. With vertical drops on the remaining sides of the castle the site must have been considered virtually impregnable. There are not a lot of buildings to see, but the climb and the views certainly make it worthwhile.

Blue John collectors will find the jewellery shops easily enough. Real enthusiasts should visit the **Ollerenshaw Collection** of Blue John in the Cavendish House Museum. Here the stone is portrayed in beautiful ornaments which were cut when the stone was more plentyful. If you are contemplating buying a Blue John ring, it is worth remembering that the stone is not that hard and may be scratched by steel or items with a similar hardness.

Castleton is particularly well known for its caverns. Strictly speaking all but one were mines. **Peak Cavern** in the village itself is the largest cave system in the Peak, extending well beyond the portion to which visitors are admitted. The entrance cavern is truly impressive: 330ft in length, over 100ft wide and 60ft high. At one time a row of cottages stood in the cave, and the remains of the former hemp rope makers craft can still be seen. There is a second cave — the Great Cave — of a similar cross section but about half the length. Peak Cavern has been receiving visitors since at least the eighteenth century and Queen Victoria made the trip in 1842.

The other three caverns are all situated out of the village and in close proximity to each other.

The **Blue John Mine** is actually quite a distance (2 miles) now that the former main road has been abandoned. To reach it, one has to take the car up the Winnats Pass, turn to the right and follow the sign-

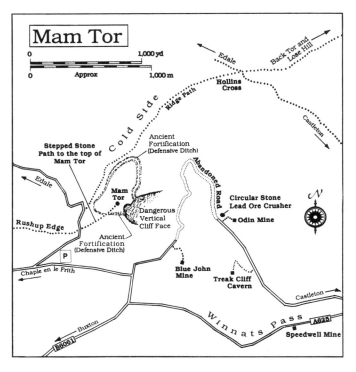

Mam Tor

0   1,000 yd

0   Approx   1,000 m

Edale

Back Tor and Lose Hill

Hollins Cross

Ridge Path

Cold Side

Castleton

Stepped Stone Path to the top of Mam Tor

Ancient Fortification (Defensive Ditch)

Abandoned Road

Edale

Mam Tor

Circular Stone Lead Ore Crusher

Odin Mine

Dangerous Vertical Cliff Face

Rushup Edge

Ancient Fortification (Defensive Ditch)

P

Blue John Mine

Treak Cliff Cavern

Castleton

Chaple en le Frith

Winnats Pass

A625

Buxton

Speedwell Mine

B6061

posts down the former main road. In the mine a considerable number of steps have to be descended, past old miners workings, shafts and a small collection of abandoned tools. There is a small amount of Blue John stone to be seen, but not a lot! However, it gives a very good idea of what an old mine working looks like and is worth the trip and steps!

On the same hillside and nearer to Castleton is **Treak Cliff Cavern** a natural cave system discovered during mining operations. It has a cave with a lot of stalactites and stalagmites which are particularly attractive.

At the foot of the Winnats Pass is the **Speedwell Mine**. Although developed as a lead mine, it was receiving visitors almost as soon as work started in 1771! The interest arose from its underground canal which was used for transportation and which is still used to convey visitors to the Bottomless Pit, extending 140ft in height and a further 70ft below the canal. Today visitors descend 104 steps to reach the electronically operated boat, which silently propels you along the low roofed channel.

It would be a pity to visit the Castleton area and yet miss the views from **Mam Tor**. Take the road up the Winnats Pass in the direction of Chapel-en-le-Frith and Whaley Bridge. At the top of the hill (it is a very steep hill too), turn right, then left and look for the car park on the right. Above is Mam Tor. There are steps up towards the top, recently completed by the National Trust. Look out for the remains of the Iron Age defensive ditch, which is crossed by the stepped pathway. Below the Hope Valley stretches away and to the north, the view is across the Vale of Edale to the southern edge of Kinder Scout.

Mam Tor sits on an old packhorse route along the ridge. It is now a well defined footpath. This may be used to create a circular route including Edale or Castleton, using the Ordnance Survey Dark Peak map. The front cover of this book shows the ridge route from Mam Tor, looking towards Lose Hill. In the mid distance is Hollins Cross, where the Edale-Castleton path crosses the ridge. Even if a circular route does not form part of your plans, a wander along the ridge (in either direction) brings memorable views of the district.

Accommodation

There is no shortage of accommodation. One way of staying in this area is to attend one of the many and varied courses held at Losehill Hall. The hall is just outside the village. Castleton Hall in the market place is a youth hostel. For more information ☎ (0433) 20235.

Places to Eat
There are plenty of tea rooms and pubs in the village and surrounding area.

 Toilets
In Castleton village, by the car park.

i **Tourist Information Centre**
Castleton
Castle Street
☎ (0433) 20679

Recommended Attractions

Blue John Cavern and Blue John Mine
Buxton Road, Castleton, near Sheffield S30 2WP
☎ (0433) 20638/20642
Open: spring, summer and autumn, daily 9.30am-6pm
(or dusk); for winter hours ☎ (0443) 20642.
World-famous source of Blue John stone for over 200
years. Free parking for cars and coaches.

Chestnut Centre
Castleton, Chapel-en-le-Frith Road (A625) near turning
for Edale
Open: daily 10.30am-5.30pm.
Country park, otter haven and owl sanctuary.

Losehill Hall
Details of courses available from the Principal Peak
National Park Study Centre, Losehill Hall, Castleton,
near Sheffield ☎ (0433) 20373.

Mam Tor
Local landmark. Part of a long ridge between the Edale
and Hope valleys. An Iron Age fort existed on the top
and its defensive ditch may be easily seen from a
distance.

Ollerenshaw Collection
(The Cavendish House Museum)
Cross Street, Castleton
☎ *(0433) 20642*
*Open: daily, 9.30am-6pm (dusk in winter) except 25
and 26 December and 1 January.*
*Adjoining the original Blue John Stone Craft Shop.
Private museum of Derbyshire treasures, including one
of the largest and finest collections of Blue John stone.*

Peak Cavern
Castleton
☎ *(0433) 20285*
*Open: Easter to end October, daily, 10am-5pm.
Closed Mondays in low season.*

Peveril Castle
(English Heritage)
☎ *(0433) 20613*
*Open: mid-October to mid-March, Monday to Saturday
9.30am-4pm, Sunday 2-4pm.*
*Norman castle founded in 1068. Steep climb up, but
magnificent views.*

Pony Trekking
At Lady Booth, near Edale
☎ *(0433) 70205*

Speedwell Cavern
Winnats Pass, Castleton
☎ *(0433) 20512*
*Open: daily, 10am-6pm throughout the year.
Visitors travel by boat along flooded mine level to
natural cavern.*

The Hope Chest
Hope village
Crafts, fashions, food and a good selection of books.

Treak Cliff Cavern
³/₄ mile west of Castleton on the A625.
☎ (0433) 20571
Open: all year except 25 December.
Richest known visible veins of Blue John with fine
displays of stalagmites and stalactites.

Hartington

The village is situated on the B5054 between Warslow
and Newhaven. It is also a couple of miles off the A515
Buxton to Ashbourne road.

Hartington can seem overwhelmed with tourists,
particularly at a weekend, although a new car park in
Mill Lane has helped to relieve congestion in the
Market Place. With its souvenir shops and tea rooms it
caters for many car bound visitors. However, it is also
the centre for the northern end of the limestone dales
on the River Dove and there is a marvellous network of
footpaths centred on the village.

Hartington is situated where Hartington Dale
reaches the broad river meadows of the River Dove. It
is probable that there was originally a stream (the
River Harden) flowing across what is now the Market
Place, but it now flows through a culvert beneath the
road surface. The stream may be seen flowing through
'The Stanner' (an opening on the culvert) at the head of
Factory Lane and close to the village Mere or
duckpond. The Mere possibly dates from the seventeenth century.

The oldest buildings (except for the church) date
from the early years of the seventeenth century.
Hartington Hall dating from 1611 is probably the
earliest complete surviving house although a previous
building existed upon the site. Many properties in the
district were rebuilt in stone during the seventeenth

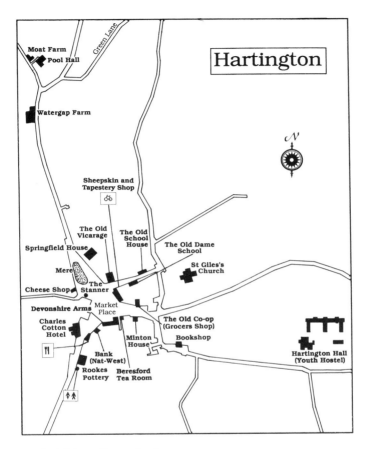

Hartington

and eighteenth centuries.

A good proportion of the older buildings have datestones and together with the variety of styles of venacular architecture make a wander around the village worthwhile. Look out particularly for the arcaded front of the **village shop** at one time The Volunteer Inn and later, the Co-op. It was orginally built as a shop in 1836 and has an unusual carving on its façade. It displays a man holding a set of scales and flanked by two women. To the right of the shop is a row of low terraced houses with the datestone '1777 T & JC'. They were built by Thomas and Jane Cantrell as cotton workers cottages. Their cotton mill was directly opposite on the site of Minton House. Several houses were faced with cut limestone blocks with gritstone used for door and window surrounds. The **Charles Cotton Hotel** is interesting in this respect as a comparison may be made with the style of the extension, which has the datestone 1864 tucked under the ridge on the gable end.

Clearly some of the houses were built to reflect the status of the occupier. For example Hartington Hall was occupied by the Bateman family until 1934, when it was let to the Youth Hostel Association, who finally purchased the hall and farm in 1951 for £4,000.

Adjacent to The Old Vicarage and the Mere is **Springfield House**, a well proportioned house, now the focus of many photographs. This was built in 1790 on earlier foundations and is very similar to **Watergap Farm** in Dig Street. The latter is dated 1766 at the front and 1693 on the smaller building at the rear. Beyond Watergap Farmhouse is Pool Hall and Moat Farm. The latter includes traces of a medieval house which formerly existed within a moat on this site. Church Street has a couple of old schools, one dated 1758 (see map of village) as well as **The Old Vicarage** at the market place end of the street. The building was originally built by the Duke of Devonshire for the manager of the Ecton Copper Mine, Cornelius Flint. The Duke owned much of the village and his son's title is the Marquis of Hartington. Many houses in the village are of no special appeal individually. Collectively however, they create street scenes of great charm and character, helping to contribute to the reputation of this justly popular village.

Situated on the hillside above the community it serves sits **St Giles' Church.** It dates from the late

Hartington Hall is now a youth hostel

thirteenth century and contains remnants of early wall
paintings. The village was well established when the
church was built. It was mentioned in the Domesday
Book and the market rights were granted by King John
in 1203 — the first in the Peak District. **Hartington
Hall**, situated near the top of Hall Bank was orginally
built in 1350 as a priory of the nuns of St Clare. The
church had been conferred upon the order in 1291, so
persumably it had been completed by this date. Bonnie
Prince Charles is alleged to have slept here on his
retreat from Derby, although in reality one wonders
whether he or one of his generals was actually quar-
tered here. The small panelled room where he is
supposed to have slept still survives. The present
house was built in 1611 in the popular local style with
projecting side wings. The sides and rear were added in
1861.

The farm buildings were also added in 1859. The bay
windows to the ground and first floor were added on
the west side in 1911, 300 years after the front was
built. Today the hall is the oldest surviving youth

hostel in the Peak District. The German founder of the youth hostelling movement, Richard Shirmann, planted the copper beech by the drive in 1934.

Accommodation
Charles Cotton Hotel; Minton House; Bank House Guest House are all in the Market Place. Self catering accommodation is available at Mrs Wain, Knowl Cottage, Market Place. The youth hostel at Hartington Hall offers a variety of private rooms with ensuite facilities for families. These are chiefly in the old barn at the rear of the hall. Meals are provided or a self catering kitchen is available.
☎ (0298) 84223

Car Park
Mill Lane.

Places to Eat
There are several tea rooms, restaurants etc, in the village.

Toilets
Adjacent to Rookes Pottery in Mill Lane.

Tourist Information Centre
Hartington
Railway Station
No telephone
Open: Easter to September. Saturday, Sunday and Bank Holiday Mondays.

Recommended Attractions

Cheese Shop
Factory Lane
Hartington
A variety of cheeses including Hartington Blue and White Stiltons.

Cycle Hire
A.J. & M. Sears
Market Place, Hartington, Buxton
☎ (0298) 84459
Open: daily, except during January and February then weekends only.

Hartington Signal Box
Preserved signal box on old railway line, now the Tissington Trail. The **Tourist Information Centre** *is here.*

Rookes Pottery
Mill Lane, Hartington, Buxton
☎ (0298) 84650
Open: weekdays 9am-5pm, Saturday 10am-5pm, Sunday 11am-5pm. Closed weekends in January and February.
Terracotta garden pottery made on the premises. Visitors may look round the workshop and see pots in production.

Sheepskin and Tapestry Shop
Lots of good clothes and souvenirs.

Hathersage

Hathersage is now a quiet commuter town on the banks of the River Derwent and below Stanage Edge which dominates the eastern skyline. It is now the only town in the National Park to possess a railway station. However its claims to fame run deeper than this. Here Samuel Fox of Bradwell, the inventor of the umbrella (as we know it) started to manufacture them at the Atlas Mill. In the churchyard, a gravestone marks the last resting place of Little John, Robin Hood's friend. Charlotte Brontë knew the village and used it as the source for *Jane Eyre*, calling it 'Morton'. Charlotte Brontë stayed at The Vicarage for 3 weeks in 1845. Her schoolfriend Ellen Nussey was sister of the vicar, Henry Nussey. St John Rivers was modelled on Henry, who had previously proposed to her. The use of the name Eyre will have been noted as a Hathersage family name. Moor House was probably Moor Seats, situated about $\frac{1}{2}$ mile north-west of the church. North Lees Hall could have been borne in mind when Charlotte wrote of Thornfield Hall, but anything else is speculation.

Hathersage grew with the development of its needle and other wire industries and millstone manufacture. The former was a dreadful occupation. The dust given off from the grinding stones caused Grinder's Disease and killed many of the employees before they were 30 years old. Today there is little evidence of its industrial development in the town. The quarries upon Stanage Edge and adjacent edges above the valley are littered with abandoned millstones. However, there must be hundreds stacked up at Bole Hill Quarry alone (see page 70).

The centre of Hathersage is the area around The George Hotel. Just to the right of it an old gritstone cheese press has been preserved. There is a good outdoor shop on the opposite side of the road, a craftshop and various places offering refreshments.

St Michael's Church is tucked away to the north of the main street. It is off the old packhorse road that climbed up the edge in the direction of Sheffield — a reminder of this being the Scotsman's Pack Inn at the bottom of Church Bank. The church was built in 1381,

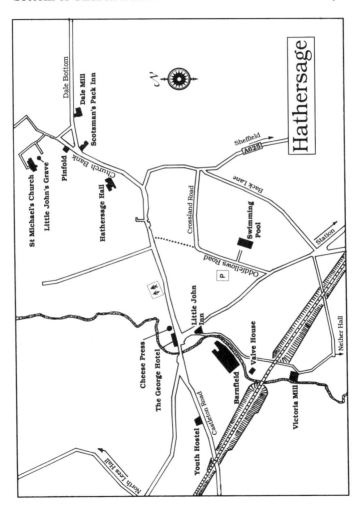

but was much restored in the last century. It has a north chancel chapel added by the Eyre family in 1463. Look out for the fifteenth-century brasses to the Eyre family. The east window and its coloured glass was added as late as 1949. It was brought here from Derwent Church, before the latter was demolished during the construction of Ladybower Reservoir. All this competes with the other fascination of the church. The grave of Little John can be found at the edge of the churchyard near to the south porch.

The lane up to the church passes the pinfold on the left, behind a high wall opposite the Scotsman's Pack Inn. Look for the tall gate to the right of the noticeboard.

On the village side of the pinfold is **Hathersage Hall**, built in 1820 with much older parts behind. It probably stands on the site of the first hall built by John Eyre in 1496. Opposite the hall the valley, known as Dale Bottom directs one's eye over Dale Mill and up towards the moors and the southern end of Stanage Edge. **Dale Mill** was used for making needles. Of more interest perhaps was Atlas Mill in Castleton Road, just beyond the George Hotel but on the opposite side of the road on the site of the Catholic schools. Here Samuel Fox was employed. In 1847 he took out a patent for umbrella frames and today's umbrellas are still made with a 'Fox Frame'. Fox left in 1847 for Sheffield and eventually established his own works at Stocksbridge.

A short walk is recommended around the village. Starting opposite the George Hotel, walk down Mill Lane at the brookside, taking the lane to the right of the Little John Inn. It passes the rear of **Bamfield Works** still complete with its stone built chimney. This was a manufactury for needles and pins and was built in 1811. Just before the railway arches are reached is a stone structure with an oval roof. It is a **valve house** on the pipeline from Derwent Reservoir. The only building still standing beneath the waters of

Ladybower Reservoir. At Derwent village there is a valve house like this one. Just past the railway line is a low building which is all that remains of the **Victoria Mill** built in 1820 for the production of needles and pins. Here the lane turns to the left away from the brook. It passes the gate to Nether Hall (built in 1838) before passing under the railway again. Upon reaching the main road, turn left and then right into Oddfellows Road. When the road turns to the right, a path continues ahead to the main street. Just out of the town on the Grindleford road on the old gasworks site is a modern cutlery factory which has received several architectural awards. The circular design was dictated by the fact that the foundations of the gasholder were too expensive to remove.

Stanage Edge is very popular with climbers

Accommodation
Youth Hostel
Castleton Road
☎ (0433) 50493

Craft Shops
'Outside', for crafts, clothes and books.
Hathersage Craft Shop
Both are in the main street.

Sports Facilities
Swimming pool off Oddfellows Road

Places to Eat
Taverna Rusticana; Longlands Eating House;
The Corner Cupboard; The George Hotel;
Country Fayre Tearoom — all in the main
street.

Recommended Attractions

Carl Wark
Iron Age hillfort situated above Padley Gorge. Has a huge platform built of gritstone blocks up to 5ft across, and ramparts 10ft high.

Derwent Dams
Three large reservoirs, Ladybower, Derwent and Howden, situated above the village of Bamford. Cycle hire centre at Fairholme, below Derwent Dam. There is a road up Derwent Dale on the west side of the reservoirs, but limited vehicular access above Fairholme. Footpath down eastern side of the lakes to the Ashopton viaduct on the A57. Footpath above Howden Reservoir to Slippery Stones where the packhorse bridge from the drowned village of Derwent has been re-erected.

The Gritstone Edges
These are a prominent geological feature east of the River Derwent. Outstanding examples are Birchen Edge, Gardom's Edge, Baslow Edge, Curbar Edge, Froggatt Edge, Millstone Edge, Burbage Edge and Stanage Edge. There are paths along the tops of most of these edges and all give spectacular views. Many are popular with rock climbers. On Birchen Edge is Nelson's Monument, erected in 1810 by a local man, while Baslow Edge has a monument to Wellington, erected in 1866. Near to Nelson's Monument are three huge rocks looking like ships with the names Victory, Defiant, and Royal Soverin [sic] on their bows. Most unusual in an area so far from the sea.

Ilam

Ilam (pronouced 'eye-lamb') is situated on the River Manifold and can be reached from the Ashbourne-Leek road (via Blore) or the Ashbourne-Buxton road (via Thorpe).

The village was remodelled by the Watts-Russell family in the early years of the nineteenth century. Today the village, standing close to the southern entrance to Dovedale is very popular and there is a country park around Ilam Hall.

Ilam Hall was rebuilt between 1821 and 1826 by Jesse Watts-Russell in the fashionable Tudor Gothic style with battlements, huge chimney stacks and flag tower. It was a large house replacing a much smaller and simpler manor house and passed by sale to the Hanbury family in 1872. For a short period earlier in the twentieth century it was used as a hotel. In 1934 the house and 1,000 acres of land were put up for sale once more. Sir Robert MacDougal purchased tracts of land in Dovedale and presented them to the National

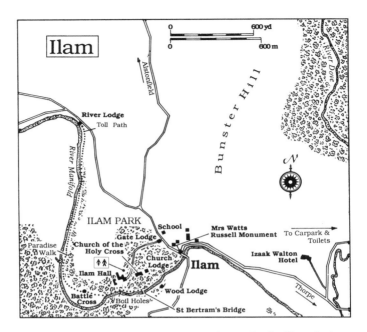

Trust. He was pursuaded to purchase the hall and give it the Youth Hostels Association 'for the perpetual use of the youth of the world'. The YHA, lacking a trust body of its own at that time, gave the building to the National Trust, but pulled down the formal quarters. Consequently all that remains are the entrance hall and armoury plus the servants' quarters. The YHA has recently spent considerable sums of money refurbishing the hall and creating a suite of private bedrooms for families who wish to stay in this lovely area.

A series of woodland walks have been established by the National Trust and these are delightful, complimenting the lovely grounds to the hall. Indeed the path along the valley floor has been known since Victorian times as **Paradise Walk**. It is best approached by walking through the arches beyond the car park in front of the house and descending the tower steps. The path descends to the river where first the River Manifold and then the River Hamps may be seen bubbling up from underground passages. Further along from the 'boil holes' the Battle Cross may be seen. This is a Victorian name given to a large Celtic cross which was found when the village was rebuilt. The path continues to a footbridge, replacing a small suspension bridge destroyed by a falling tree in 1962. Upstream from here is **River Lodge**, one of four lodges to the hall. An inscribed stone states that it was laid in 1840 by Jemima, Countess of Monteglas. She was the daughter of Jesse Watts-Russell.

A magnificent carving of Jemima's grandfather may be seen in the **Church of the Holy Cross**. Carved by

How Ilam Hall once looked

Sir Francis Chantrey in 1831, it shows the old man, David Pike Watts, giving his last blessing to his daughter and her children. It is a poignant composition expressing great sensitivity. There are several other interesting features in the church. To the right of the entrance is a blocked Saxon doorway. A chapel on the south side which was built in 1618 contains the tomb of St Bertelin and an alabaster effigy of Robert Meverell and his wife (1686). They lived at the nearby Throwley Hall. Look out also for the Norman font, maiden's gloves and two crosses in the churchyard.

Below the church is **St Bertram's Bridge**. It is a former packhorse bridge and was the old way into Ilam village. When the model village was built, a new bridge was constructed lower downstream. A spring may be seen close to the old bridge. The latter continued to serve as one of the drives to the hall. **Wood Lodge** stands where the woodland gives way to pasture, downstream from the old bridge. **Church Lodge**, which is close to the church and by a huge yew tree is presumably one of the former village houses. The other lodge stands by the main drive entrance and is known as **Gate Lodge**.

Behind Gate Lodge is the lovely village **school** with the master's house beyond it. The centre piece of the village is the village cross, built by Jesse Watts-Russell in 1840 in memory of his first wife Mary. It is based upon the Eleanor Crosses. Unfortunately the delicately carved cross on the top came off in the 1962 gales and a plain finial was used as a replacement.

Ilam retains several mysteries. The first is the location of the old village. One would expect it to be near the church. The water course near St Bertram's Bridge could have originally been the village well. A lot of drainage pipes have been located on the caravan park by the hall but their purpose is unknown. Is this where the village was? Also in medieval times the village had a corn mill but no trace of this can be found and its pond presumably disappeared when the hall and grounds were remodelled. Despite the popularity of the country park, this is a lovely area and well worth exploring, especially if you follow the various paths through the park.

 Accommodation
You may stay at the youth hostel at Ilam Hall. Booking is advisable (☎ Thorpe Cloud 212). Modern family bedrooms have been recently added if you do not like dormitories. Cafeteria or small self-catering kitchen is available.

 Places to Eat
The nearby high class Izaak Walton Hotel has a small side room with a food bar ideal for ramblers and adults with young children. In Thorpe, there is a pub and The Peveril of the Peak Hotel (Trust House Forte).

Ilam Hall and Country Park
With car park (there is a charge except for National Trust members), plus toilets, National Trust shop and Information Centre (☎ Thorpe Cloud 245) and picnic areas.

Tea room (not National Trust) behind the hall in the old stable block.

Monyash and Magpie Mine

Monyash is a small, compact village of limestone built houses founded prior to the Domesday Book of 1086 (where it is referred to as *Maneis*). Its dependency upon agriculture was overtaken by lead mining interests and formerly a lead miners' Barmoot Court used to meet here — the oldest industrial court in the country. The core of the village is still the area around the village green. A market was held here every Tuesday. Monyash was the last Peakland village to obtain a market charter in 1340. It also had the right to a fair which was held over 3 days at the Feast of Trinity in July.

Monyash had four meres (ponds) but only the large **Fere Mere** now survives. The village also had two pumps for drinking water. However, this was spring water and very hard and so housewives used to prefer the softer water of Fere Mere for daily usage. Between this and the school was **Cow Mere**. By mutual arrangement the farmers drove their cattle here to drink — a different time was set aside for each herd. Then, when the field work was finished later in the day, the horses were taken for a drink. How different the village is nowadays. The tranquil practices of the past are a long way from the busy traffic of today.

Reflected in the waters of Fere Mere is the spire of the **church**. Dedicated to St Leonard, it was founded about 1198. Pevsner's *Buildings of Derbyshire* also tells us that contemporary with this date are the chancel arch, the south doorway and lower part of the tower. Just after the village received its market charter, the south transept was built. The village was already an important lead ore producer and the local miners had already found it necessary to seek confirmation of their ancient rights before an inquest held in Ashbourne in 1288. It is thought that the parish chest, bound with iron for safety, dates from about this time too. Within

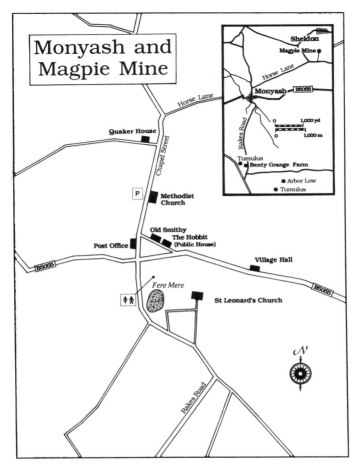

Monyash and Magpie Mine

Quaker House

Horse Lane

Chapel Street

P

Methodist Church

Old Smithy

The Hobbit (Public House)

Post Office

B5055

Village Hall

B5055

Fere Mere

St Leonard's Church

Rakes Road

N

Sheldon

Magpie Mine

Horse Lane

Monyash — B5055

Rakes Road

0   1,000 yd

0   1,000 m

Tumulus

Benty Grange Farm

Arbor Low

Tumulus

the churchyard lies Sir Maurice Oldfield. Britain's spy master 'M' in the James Bond films was based upon him, as was Smiley in John Le Carré's *Tinker Tailor Soldier Spy*. He was born at Over Haddon and went to school at Bakewell. This small and relatively simple church affords a haven for quiet reflection in a busy village.

Much of the village social life features around the village hall and The Hobbit pub, better remembered by many as The Bull's Head. Adjacent to the pub the old smithy is now a tool hire shop with camping gas and other supplies for tourists. Monyash also has a small grocery shop and post office but no picnic tables except for the patrons of the pub.

Around the corner in **Chapel Street** is a small car park on the site of **Jack Mere**, just before the Methodist chapel. This mere often dried up in hot weather and flooded across the road when it was very wet. Beyond the car park is the youth club in an old Quaker meeting house built in 1711. Chapel Street was formerly part of an important packhorse road which turned to the right along Horse Lane, heading for Ashford-in-the-Water and its bridge across the River Wye. There is some speculation as to whether the little cottage at the junction with **Horse Lane** was a toll house. A little further up the Taddington road on the left is the pinfold built to hold stray animals and recently restored.

Horse Lane leads towards Sheldon and also **Magpie Mine**. Upon reaching a T-junction, turn right and on drawing level with the mine buildings, a track gives access to the complex. Mining finished here in 1958 and the majority of the tips are grassed over. In May and June the area is a haven for yellow pansies, thyme, ox-eye daisies, birds foot trefoil and many other plants. Also found growing here is the spring sandwort, a tiny white flower which is especially lead tolerant. The flowers are protected and should not be touched.

The mine buildings are the only major complex of its type in the Peak to have survived from the last century. It is rather impressive with its large engine house, chimneys, head gear and other buildings, including the field headquarters of the Peak District Mines Historical Society. There are many old shafts in this area and although the open and deep ones are

The impressive remains of Magpie Mine

capped for safety, they should be treated with respect
and all depressions avoided. A guide book on the mine
is available at the Peak District Lead Mining Museum
at Matlock Bath.

Returning to Monyash, to the south of the village a
relic of prehistory may be visited. This is the stone
circle of **Arbor Low**. From the Green, take Rakes
Road past Fere Mere and out of the village. The road
climbs up onto the limestone plateau in the direction of
Parsley Hay. At a sharp bend about a mile or so from
the village is Benty Grange Farm. On the hillside
behind it (just out of sight) is a burial mound or
tumulus. In 1848 a helmet of a Christian Saxon warrior was found here and is now kept at Sheffield
Museum. Continuing down the road the turn to the left
leads towards Youlgreave. The first farm track to the
right may be taken to reach Arbor Low. It is possible to
park at the farm and there is a charge for access. Walk
between the farm buildings to a stile which gives
access to a field; turn left and walk uphill and over

another stile to reach the henge. This huge circular monument is Neolithic and 250ft in diameter. There are a total of 46 large stones and 13 smaller ones, with 4 additional stones in the middle. The stones were originally vertical and are surrounded by a ditch and external bank 6ft high.

A little to the west and visible across the adjacent field is **Gib Hill**, of a similar age but with a Bronze Age burial chamber on the top of it. It is the largest barrow in the Peak and was excavated in 1848. A stone cist or chamber was found containing an urn and a cremation. The views from these monuments stretch to distant horizons so take your camera!

 Accommodation
Lathkill Dale Hotel at Over Haddon offers accommodation. For more information
☎ Bakewell 814768

P **Car Park**
Near the chapel in Chapel Street.

Places to Eat
Monyash has The Hobbit pub and the Lathkill Dale Hotel at Over Haddon is also recommended. There is also a quaint tea room in Over Haddon's Main Street.

 Toilets
Rakes Road, adjacent to Fere Mere.

Recommended Attraction

Magpie Mine
Sheldon
Mining remains visible from the road. The Peak District Mining Museum at Matlock Bath runs guided tours on occasions around the site. For more information contact the museum ☎ (0629) 583834. The latter is

open daily except Christmas Day (later closing in summer). The remains include a Cornish-type engine house with chimneys, remains of a steam whim, more recent head gear last used in 1958 and a replica horse whim. A footpath runs through the site.

Wirksworth

This old lead mining and quarrying town has a lot of interest. It houses what is probably the oldest industrial court in Britain and was formerly the third town of Derbyshire. Its importance grew on its extractive industries and it now hosts the National Stone Museum. Near the latter is one of Britain's largest limestone mines which produces very pure stone used in sugar manufacture. Its early textile connections included Sir Richard Arkwright who built Haarlem

The houses pictured here are at the rear of the main street in Wirksworth

Wirksworth

Cromford and National Stone Centre
Old Lock Up (Now Private House)
Greenhill
Harrison Drive
Moot Hall
Chapel Lane
Babington House
The Dale
Red Lion Inn
1-3 Greenhill
P
North End
Ashbourne
Coldwell Street
The Old Manor House
Town Hall
Heritage Centre
The Manse
West End
Market Place
St Mary's Church
P
Bede Alms House
Antony Gell Grammer School
Yokecliffe Lane
Cruck Building (Remains)
The Gate House
Derby
N

Mill on the road to Derby.

It retains much of its past, despite the loss of some very old properties comparatively recently. There seems to be no shortage of narrow passageways worth exploring. It has a very active Civic Society. Interest in its heritage is reflected in the publication of two separate town trails, the Civic Society publication perhaps being the best.

The focal point of Wirksworth is the **church**. Its foundation dates back to perhaps the seventh century, although the current building dates from the thirteenth century. It houses a superb Saxon stone-carved coffin lid considered to be of national importance. In the south transept is a Saxon carving of a miner, although the stone was found at Bonsall.

As in Ashbourne, there has been much encroachment on the **Market Place** and this accounts for the properties which now separate it from the churchyard. The Hope and Anchor pub and its adjacent properties down to The Causeway also stand in the old Market Place which stretched up to the **Red Lion Hotel**. Built in

1770, this coaching inn still retains a much older (possibly medieval) chimney at the side. Across the road is another eighteenth-century building. Around the corner **1-3 Greenhill** has recently been saved. This seventeenth-century building was a shell until work began in 1981. Further up the lane is **Babington House**, of similar age. To the west of Greenhill is The Dale and an area known as **The Puzzle Gardens**. It is a jumble of little cottages worth exploring.

To the right of the Red Lion Inn is Coldwell Street with the Italianate Town Hall on the corner, built in 1871. Almost opposite is the United Reform Church. This stands on the side of Chapel Lane. Along here on the left is the **Moot Hall**, built in 1814. This houses the Barmoot Court, which meets twice a year. The jury of twenty-four people still receive a clay pipe and tobacco when it meets! The miners' standard measuring dish, which dates from 1513, is kept in the hall. At the end of Chapel Lane is the **Old Lock Up**. D.H. Lawrence rented Mountain Cottage at Middleton-by-Wirksworth during World War I. His wife Frieda (née Richthofen) was of German birth and had to report here weekly.

Returning to Coldwell Street, look out for The Gables on the left and The Manse on the right. By taking **Blind Lane** one returns towards the church. On the right is the old Anthony Gell Grammar School founded in 1576 and rebuilt in a neo-Gothic style in 1828. The building is now used for furniture manufacture. The school is probably the oldest surviving school in the Peak. Gell also had a row of almshouses built nearby. They were completed after his death and still survive. The town retains its church clipping ceremony, when people surround the church holding hands. It is held on the Sunday following the 8 September. Wirksworth has a market on Tuesdays and observes its well dressing ceremony on the Whitsun Bank Holiday.

Places to Eat
At various inns. It also has a restaurant (Raffles), The Bistro in St John Street and The Crown Yard Kitchen next to Heritage Centre.

Car Parks
Off Coldwell Street and in the Market Place.

Toilets
Off St John Street and off Coldwell Street.

Recommended Attractions

Black Rocks Trail
Bolehill, near Wirksworth. Three Forestry Commission trails of 1, $1^1/_2$ and 2 miles length.

The Gallery
4 West End, Wirksworth. ☎ (0629) 823557.
Open: April to end December, Thursday, Friday and Saturday 10.30am-5pm; January, February and March, Saturdays only. Also open by appointment. Paintings, original prints, ceramics, glass.

Middleton Top Winding Engine House
Signposted off the B5036 Cromford to Wirksworth road ☎ (0629) 823204. Open: Easter to October, 10.30am-5pm, Sundays (engine static); first Saturday in month and Bank Holidays (engine operating). Restored beam engines built in 1829 by the Butterley Company.

National Stone Centre
Middleton-by-Wirksworth
☎ (0629) 824833
Open: 10am-5pm through the year.
Set in an old quarry near the Cromford and High Peak railway line, now the High Peak Trail. Shop, light refreshments and toilets available.

Shows and Events

T he list below includes the majority of those events occuring annually in the area. Some occur over the end of one month and the beginning of the next and are listed twice. It is important to realise that there are many events which are not included but which may be of interest. These include the occasional steaming days at Leawood Pump House, festivals at Haddon Hall and Chatsworth House; local village events such as church festivals and the antique fairs at Hartington village hall; talks and organised rambles.

A full list of events is published in the free magazine, the *Peakland Post*, published by the National Park.

Early spring
Ashbourne Shrovetide Football — Shrove Tuesday and Ash Wednesday.
Flagg Races (High Peak Hunt Point to Point) Tuesday after Easter.

May
Alstonfield Horse Show and Gymkhana
Ashford-in-the-Water Well Dressing
Bamford Sheep Dog Trials
Castleton Garland Ceremony 28 May
 (Oak Apple Day)
Chatsworth Angling Fair
Endon Well Dressing
Etwall Well Dressing

Leek Arts Festival
Leek May Fair
Middleton-by-Youlgreave Well Dressing
Monyash Well Dressing
Pott Shrigley — Rose Queen fête
Tissington Well Dressing — Ascension Day until
  following Monday
Winster Market Fair, Bank Holiday Monday
Wirksworth Well Dressing

*Dressed well
for the
occasion at
Tissington*

June
Ashford Well Dressing
Bakewell Well Dressing and Carnival week including
  raft race on River Wye
Chelmorton Well Dressing
Grindleford Carnival

Hope Well Dressing and Wakes
Litton Well Dressing
Monyash Well Dressing
Rowsley Well Dressing and Festival
Tideswell Well Dressing and Wakes Carnival
Winster Wakes
Youlgreave Well Dressing

July
Alport Love Feast
Ashbourne Carnival
Bakewell Well Dressing and Carnival week
Bamford Carnival
Baslow Well Dressing
Bradwell Well Dressing and Gala week
Buxton International Arts Festival
Buxton Well Dressing
Chesterfield Medieval Market
Glossop Carnival
Hollinsclough village fête
Hope Well Dressing and Wakes
Leek Club Day (Sunday school and other
  organisations procession)
Leek Show
Litton Well Dressing
Lyme Park Festival
Padley Pilgrimage
Pilsley Well Dressing
Stoney Middleton Well Dressing
Tideswell Well Dressing
Winster Wakes

August
Ashbourne Show
Ashover Show
Bakewell Show
Bradwell Well Dressing and Gala week
Chesterfield Market (Bank Holiday)

Crich Tramway Museum, Grand Transport
 Extravaganza
Cromford Steam Rally
Dovedale Sheepdog Trials
Eyam Well Dressing
Foolow Well Dressing
Froggatt Show
Grindleford Show
Hope Show
Hucklow and District Wakes
Ipstones Show
Leek Carnival
Lyme Park Festival
Lyme Sheepdog Trials
Macclesfield Forest Chapel Rush Bearing
Manifold Valley Show
Wormhill Well Dressing

September

Chatsworth Country Fair
Eyam Well Dressing
Foolow Well Dressing
Hartington Sports
Hartington Well Dressing
Holme Valley Torchlight Procession
Jenkin Chapel, Saltersford Harvest Thanksgiving
Longnor Well Dressing and Sports
Longshaw Sheepdog Trials
Lyme Park Horse Trials
Matlock Bath Illuminations and Firework Display
Penistone Show
Wormhill Well Dressing

Index

127

A Note to the Reader

Thank you for buying this book, we hope it has helped you to enjoy your stay in the Peak District. We have worked hard to produce a guidebook which is as accurate as possible. With this in mind, any comments, suggestions or useful information you may have would be appreciated. Those who send in the most helpful letters will be credited in future editions.

Please send your letters **Freepost** to:

Tonya Monk (Editor)
Moorland Publishing Co Ltd
Free Post
Ashbourne
Derbyshire
DE6 9BR

MPC The Travel Specialists